Life in Abundance

Filling Your Heart With a Deeper Understanding of God's Word

100 DEVOTIONS

MANDY SHROCK

Library of Congress Control Number: 2022914425

ISBN: 978-1-958477-00-7 (Hardcover)
ISBN: 978-1-958477-12-0 (Paperback)
ISBN: 978-1-958477-01-4 (Digital Online)

Some names have been changed to protect the privacy of those in my stories.

Front cover image by Jenneth Dyck.
Interior design by KUHN Design Group.

First printing edition 2022.

Published by In Abundance, LLC
info@marriageinabundance.com

ACKNOWLEDGEMENTS:

First, and foremost, colossal credit goes to my mom, Cindy Frost. Without her, you would not be holding this book in your hands. She was my biggest critic, per my request. I asked from her for simply a quick opinion of my first writings. Instead, she pored over every single one of them for large chunks of time and offered a wealth of feedback. She improved my writing style significantly, helped me stay organized in my thought-process, revealed to me when I was flat-out wrong, pointed out where I may come off too strong, and softened my words. She turned me into a much better writer. Mom, you deserve more credit than you have allowed me to give.

I'd, also, like to thank my father-in-law, Sonny Shrock, who motivated me to continue writing. I started writing for a small venue, never intending to publish a book. Sonny asked to read my "backstage" writings. Then he asked for more. And more. Then one day, he called me out of the blue just to tell me how proud he was of me and my writings. His words—impassioned and full of conviction—were to the uncertain author in me, a heavy rain in the desert. Sonny, your words fueled me to write this book.

Big thanks to my husband, Joel, who supports me in so many ways I can't count. He believes in me, encourages me, sacrifices financially to make my dreams a reality, brings stability to our crazy home, and challenges me to be a better human. Joel, you are a piece of God given to me. I love you more than you know. Thank you.

Big thanks to my editor, Caryn Rivadeneira, for teaching me a great deal and going above and beyond in her encouragement to me.

Contents

Introduction

The devotions in this book dig deep. To give the depth of insight into the Scriptures, many things were considered: the historical and cultural context of the writings, the meaning of words in their original language, and differing views of theologians. Then, application was given to each verse. To prevent "fluffy" devotions, they became rather lengthy. While some people may have much time in their day to spend on devotions, there are some who have only shorter amounts of time. To maintain sustenance while fitting each verse into a short devotion that accommodates each lifestyle, many of the Scripture studies of just one verse were divided among multiple devotions.

Within each devotion is a prayer. Written prayers were requested by some who want to grow in their prayer life but don't know what to say. However, if you would rather formulate your own prayers, that is highly encouraged.

Music has a way of moving knowledge from our heads into our hearts; therefore, each devotion was matched with songs pertaining to that devotion. If you have time, you can choose to worship immediately after reading the devotion. But, if you don't have the luxury of time, you can listen in the car on your way to work or while completing mindless chores during your day. Again, choose what is best for you.

I learned a great deal through writing these devotionals. Many times, I wrestled with the Word as it dug deep into my heart, shone its light at the recesses, and exposed my own flaws and failures. At times, the Word cut straight through me, and I realized, *Oh dang, I'm guilty of that!* Some of the "preaching" here is not in areas I've become proficient, but goals I'm working toward. It's a privilege to learn the truth, to have the opportunity to apply it in my own life, and to fight to become a new, improved version of myself. I'm grateful to God for his forgiveness and to my friends and family who have seen my "ugly" and offered me grace.

We can't improve our flaws if we're not willing to face them. Let's journey into our hearts together to see what God may reveal to us. Let's be transparent with each other, rip off our façades, and allow Jesus the opportunity to give what only he can give—healing to our souls. Healing comes, not in the dark, but in the Light!

1

Our Desire for Life Abundantly

The thief comes only to steal and kill and destroy.
I came that they may have life and have it abundantly.

JOHN 10:10 ESV

Life. It has left us feeling much to be desired. Because there is. We're missing something because we've been broken into and robbed. There is a thief who has come to "steal, kill, and destroy" all that God intends for us: life abundant with love, joy, and peace. This thief's crusade to rob us began in the Garden of Eden when he lied to us and we believed him, exchanging Plan A for Plan B. Plan A crumbled into ruins when mankind bit into the wrong advice, thinking there was a better way.

A little refresher course: We were created as perfect people and placed in a perfect setting, the Garden of Eden. The first two chapters of Genesis tell us of the life that was meant to be—no pain, no sorrow, no death, perfect connection with God, and perfect union with one another. But rather quickly (chapter 3), things went very wrong. Despite warning, we chose the wrong path—and God set Plan B into motion. Now we breathe, and attempt to have life, in an imperfect world of our own making, a world destroyed by greed. In the inner recesses of our hearts, we long for what we once had. It is a longing placed in each of us by God, himself. A longing he would have fulfilled perfectly in Plan A.

When sin entered the world, along came discontentment with life and hiding from God, the only One who could fill the hunger of our hearts. The longing within us cries out for more, for what was lost in the Garden, for that perfect world. Our expectations for "more" carry on. By design, we are always searching, sometimes subconsciously, for that perfect world that no longer exists.

Typically, we see dissatisfaction as a negative thing, a part of our sinful nature, but what we don't realize is that our *desire for more* is God's design for Plan B. God expects us to seek more out of life. The problem is, we displace our *desire for more* with things that don't ever satisfy, the things of this broken world. We want a bigger house, a fancier car, a higher-paying job, more vacation time, a spouse who is more romantic and bickers less, the perfect kids (you know, the ones we see so perfectly displayed on social media), and more money than we need. We compare ourselves to others who we think have "everything" until we find out Mr. & Mrs. Perfect HaveItAll are equally discontent. There is still something lacking, something lost.

The thing we lack is life, BIG LIFE, the spiritual and emotional equivalent of LIVING LARGE! This emptiness is there for a reason: that is to point us to God. We're meant to desire more life. And God is happy to oblige. He longs to satisfy!

Reflection: What unfulfilled desires plague you? In what ways do you attempt to satisfy that desire?

Prayer: Father, I know this life I'm living is not Plan A. I'm feeling it. I've been discontent and searching for more, but I usually look to the things that will never satisfy. Teach me to look to you for satisfaction. Help me understand what true, abundant life is. Fill me with all the right desires and bring me this abundant life you planned for me to have. Amen.

Worship: "Back to the Garden" by Crowder and "Let It Echo (Heaven Fall)" by Jesus Culture

2

The Thief Steals, Kills, and Destroys

The thief comes only to steal and kill and destroy. I came that they may have life and have it abundantly.

John 10:10 ESV

Our enemy, Satan the Swindler, wants what is not his, our souls. If he can't have that, he'll try to rob us of the abundant life we were meant to have.

The Greek word for *steal* is *klepto*, which is an artful way of pickpocketing undetectably. What we had is gone before we realize what happened. It's a cunning technique of thievery, unnoticed by those being robbed blind.

If Satan can't sneaky-steal it, his next maneuver is to kill. The Greek word for *kill* used in this verse is *thuo*, which is to sacrifice, to give up something that is precious. If he can't steal it, he will cunningly convince us to give it up. Adam and Eve were duped by this kind of persuasion and sometimes so are we. What looks like a slice of heaven, promising to improve our lives is, in actuality, destructive. These can be things like having an affair, cheating our way to the top, or taking revenge on another. Those tricky things that look so enticing come back to bite us in the butt with the venom of a serpent. If he can't steal God's blessings from us, he will try to convince us to forfeit them.

The third strategy of Satan is to destroy, which is from the Greek word *apollumi,* meaning to ruin or waste. If he can't steal it or convince us to hand it over, he will ruin it. This thief wants to destroy our lives, most importantly our souls and eternities with God. However, if we are in Christ, the thief cannot have our souls.

Satan is a sore loser. Dissatisfied with the off-limit status of our souls, he then robs us of the enjoyment of life here on earth. He steals our joy, our peace, and our trust in the Lord. He blinds us to the purpose of our existence and diverts our focus, so we take our eyes off Jesus. Then he dishes out to us trials, distractions, obstacles, and interruptions until, in utter discouragement and defeat, we forget who we are in Christ.

Don't let Satan get you down! Hold on tight to your faith and to the truths of the Word. Lying is Satan's go-to. Don't bite! Don't allow him to convince you to give up what he has no power to take away.

Reflection: What has the master thief stolen from you? What has he talked you into forfeiting with a convincing lie that your life would be better? What in your life has been ruined? How can you hold tight to your faith and to truth? How can you catch the enemy in his lies before you bite into them?

Prayer: Savior of my soul, I've had so much taken from me—so much stolen, sacrificed and ruined. I've been lied to and told to believe I am not valuable to you. The enemy wants me to give up my faith and the abundant life you gave me. He wants to take what you created me to desire. Help me to call it out as the lie that it is. Help me to hold tight and not allow what is mine to be stolen, given up or ruined. Amen.

Worship: "Belong To You (Enemy Can't)" by Here Be Lions and "Stand My Ground" by Zach Williams

3

Life Abundantly

The thief comes only to steal and kill and destroy. I came that they may have life and have it abundantly.

John 10:10 ESV

Let's say you are given a vacation package. You have multiple choices and they all cost you nothing. Are you going to choose the small town forty miles away, stay in the motel the police are well-acquainted with and eat at the truck stop? Or are you going to choose the package offering a private island in the Caribbean with accommodations including a luxury spa and your own private chef?

Spiritually speaking, Jesus has an offer. It is only an offer—not automatically given. His offer, "that they may have life, and have it more abundantly." "They may have" is referring to potential, to what is possible, to what is available for the taking. It's a choice we don't have to take, and some of us don't. Some of us are saved, but walking around as though dead inside, as if we've chosen the small-town motel package, not having taken advantage of the abundant life offered to us here and now.

Which package have you chosen? Do you want to live a lame life, fruitless and unsatisfying? Or do you want to take hold of the abundant, satisfying life offered to you?

Before we begin to chase after lavish homes, luxury cars, worldwide travel, and more money than we know what to do with, we need to recognize what Jesus meant by "abundant life." We learn in 1 Corinthians 1:26-29 that God's main priority for us is not monetary wealth and high position. Paradoxically, sometimes following Christ grants us more troubles. In more places in the world than we want to think about, following Christ can get us arrested or even martyred! It's obviously not a lack of problems Jesus is offering us. The abundant life is a state of being from within, not the result of external circumstances. His desire is to increase our "wealth" not monetarily, but in deep soul-satisfying ways.

Take Solomon for example. He had all the material things one could ever imagine, yet, found it all meaningless (Ecclesiastes 5:10-15). On the contrary, many others in the Bible lived lives of struggle, suffering and pain, yet were able to sing in prison, march confidently into battle with the odds stacked against them, and walk into a fiery furnace with hope. We think *we* were dealt an unfair hand in life. Many believers throughout history were tortured, imprisoned, stoned, sawed in two, destitute, treated unfairly, beaten, and homeless. Yet it was these same struggling people who spoke of a peace beyond understanding and a deep-seated joy. That is what's there for the taking. That is abundant life.

The "abundant life" Jesus offers includes: joy and peace despite circumstances; patience and wisdom to make the right choices; strength and encouragement to keep going when we're weary; the ability to see truth; freedom from the bondage of sin; rest for our souls; freedom from guilt through forgiveness; healing for our broken spirits; the ability to see good come from bad; guidance when confused; the ability to see God's hand move and work; and love and grace to extend to others who try our patience and break our hearts.

While we're temporarily detained on this broken earth—a harsh environment now operating on Plan B with indescribable brokenness—what is more valuable: depending on material things which give us a false sense of security or moving through the struggles of life with the abundancy of God-given strength, truth, and freedom?

The abundant life—it's there for the taking. We simply need to accept.

Reflection: Look back at the examples of the kind of abundant life Jesus offers. What aspects of abundant life may be lacking from your life? What steps will you take to accept this gift?

Prayer: Jesus, thank you for your gracious offer of abundant life, a life of triumph and fulfillment in this harsh place. Help me to stop chasing the things that have the false appearance of a better life but instead, leave me feeling empty. May I be radically changed and profoundly satisfied. Amen.

Worship: "Here In This Moment" by Beckah Shae and "Graves Into Gardens" by Elevation Worship

4

Deceitful Desires of Old Self

You were taught, with regard to your former way of life, to put off your old self, which is being corrupted by its deceitful desires; to be made new in the attitude of your minds; and to put on the new self, created to be like God in true righteousness and holiness.

Ephesians 4:22-24

When someone drowns, the lungs fill with water, preventing breathing. The water must be forced out of the lungs to make room for air. In a spiritual sense, our "old self," defined in our verse as our "former way of life," has been drowning us, choking the life out of us. As in physical drowning, the end result of spiritual drowning is death—death to the soul, death to abundant life. Our "former way of life" prevents us from inhaling the air we were designed to breathe, which is the very Spirit of our Creator who gives life in abundance (Genesis 2:7, Job 33:4).

When we're drowning in "deceitful desires," we don't always realize. These desires come natural to us and blend in perfectly with our cultural norm. Therefore, it takes being in the Word to run point-blank into the "old self" with a clear picture of what a "new self" should look like (Hebrews 4:12). When solving a multi-step math problem, if everything is correct except one little step, the whole answer will be wrong. Worldly thinking, our old self, is much the same. There is a great deal of truth in the world's reasoning, but it is interwoven with error and unless we're going back to the Word to find truth, we won't be able to recognize those lies concealed in truth. The lies of the world lead us to "deceitful desires."

Some examples of worldly "truth" that lead us to "deceitful desires" and end up choking us to death include thoughts such as: *I need more and more to be satisfied. It's fine to manipulate others to get what I want. I must step on others or lie to get to the top. It's okay to criticize others who do things differently than I do. It's not a big deal to treat others of a different race, gender, or religion with disrespect. Porn will gratify me and is a victimless crime. I can live above my level of income. I should retaliate against others who offend me to prevent myself from becoming a doormat. I can save face by blaming others when my own failures are brought to light.* This way of thinking points to a corrupted heart and is counter to what we were created to be. We think we're preserving and gratifying ourselves when, to the contrary, our souls are being corrupted—we're dying.

Corruption is a powerful word. When Paul says we are being corrupted by "old self ways," he is not painting a pretty picture. It's not something we can take lightly or skim over as he is not talking about socially unacceptable behavior, rather utter destruction of our souls.

There must be a change in our thinking. Our thoughts must be different than the rationality of the world, which is faulty, shadowed, and darkened with lies. The only way to recognize thoughts darkened by lies is to get a glimpse of the Light. Getting to know God will always change us. As we trust God as the final authority over right and wrong, our thoughts and attitudes change. We appear different than the world in both our actions and in the deep recesses of our hearts. It's not that our "new self" no longer has the thoughts and temptations of the "old self," but knowing and experiencing God brings awareness that the negative thoughts and temptations are a part of our "old self" and, in fact, are corrupting us. Recognizing them as "deceitful desires," we can avoid corruption by nailing our temptations to the cross and rising above with our "new self."

Reflection: In reading the third paragraph, does anything stand out as something you've bought into believing would help you? Can you identify other deceitful desires that need to be "put off" as part of the old self?

Prayer: God, thank you for your Word which enlightens me to that which drowns me and to that which brings me life more abundantly. Teach me to recognize my old self. Help me to put it off daily. Amen.

Worship: "Let It Fade" by Jeremy Camp and "Only Love Remains" by JJ Heller

5

Putting on the New Self

You were taught, with regard to your former way of life, to put off your old self, which is being corrupted by its deceitful desires; to be made new in the attitude of your minds; and to put on the new self, created to be like God in true righteousness and holiness.

EPHESIANS 4:22-24

There are some people who seem to merely exist. In a room full of people, they sit with arms-crossed and faces dead-panned, barely speaking a word. At home, they tune out the family, showing no interest in those around them. I've walked through journeys with a few of these people who then experienced life-altering events, shaking them to their core, causing them to awaken with a fresh passion and zeal for life. God worked behind-the-scenes to renovate their souls, turning the walking dead into the walking invigorated! After the Spirit awakened them, they came alive with passion for a world unseen to us. They began to feel joy for the first time ever. They felt a renewed enthusiasm for life and a new-found compassion for others. Not only did they feel the effects of the transformation, but it was also evident to everyone who knew them.

Some of us go through a dynamic transformation over a short period of time, while others experience changes on a smaller scale over a greater amount of time. Nevertheless, when we allow Christ the room to move in our hearts, we will change.

When we're made new by God's love and discipline, we become the person we were created to be. We produce the fruit of God's Spirit and are not governed by our selfish desires. Our new selves reveal God in all we do as we are a reflection of him. We have new longings to love, convictions to choose righteousness, power to live free from guilt, strength to weather the storm, capacity to understand and demonstrate compassion, loving acceptance for people different from us, determination to remain faithful when nothing makes sense. In short, we are "being made new in the attitude of our minds." We are becoming that person who was "created to be like God in true righteousness and holiness."

We don't simply sign up with Jesus, then work hard to change our actions with our own little self-improvement plan—that is legalistic and futile. Change happens, by grace through faith, so God gets all the glory, not us. God creates the new person we are to "put on." For example, without God causing the change, our legalistic self-improvement agenda would simply be slapping a fake smile over hostility—basically putting a bandage on cancer. Our Creator is the only one who can transform a heart. If we will obey, he will transform.

God offers this gift of a "new self." We are welcome to waste it and leave it in the pretty gift package. But to take advantage of it, we are required to be participants in the action and put the "new self" on. It takes motivation. It takes discipline. It takes courage, prayer, and accountability. It takes being in the Word regularly. When driving without cruise control, we occasionally check our speed. If we make it a habit, every time we see a speed-limit sign, to glance down at our speed, we keep ourselves in check. In a spiritual sense, the Word of God is a speed limit sign we pass every day.

Lastly, we are called to righteousness and holiness. God cannot tolerate sin. God and sin are incompatible, like magnets that repel. Sin cannot exist in his presence. Therefore, this "old self" full of sin drives us away from God. When we are living in sin, we are separated from God's presence and cannot hear from him (Isaiah 59:2, Micah 3:4). We must show sin the door if we want the life-changing companionship of our Maker.

Jesus is serious about sin. In Matthew 5:30, he says, "And if your hand—even your stronger hand—causes you to sin, cut it off and throw it away. It is better for you to lose one part of your body than for your whole body to be thrown into hell." Though it would seem Jesus is into self-mutilation, he is using extreme, figurative speech to help us understand the criticality of the sin. He's saying, whatever is causing you to sin needs dealt with seriously—eliminated—even if it's as painful as losing your dominant hand. If you're tempted by a certain TV show, cancel the subscription to that show's platform. If the temptation is on your phone, install an accountability app. If you're prone to drunkenness, don't hang in the company of drunk friends. If you notice you're more prone to sin when you're with your friend, Jim, don't hang out with Jim, or bring along another friend you know will encourage you to make the right choices. If you're tempted to have an affair on the job, transfer within the company or change jobs. Jesus is that serious about your purity, and he will honor your sacrifice.

To be "made new" is not to be deprived of your desires but to have life to the fullest, life more abundantly. Here's to the new "you"!

Reflection: Have you ever witnessed a soul transformation in either yourself or someone else? How can you unwrap the packaging of your "new self" and put it on? What actions can you take to guard yourself from falling into the trap of deceitful desires? How would your relationships improve if you took off the old self and put on the new?

Prayer: God, thank you for making me new through what you have done. I'm grateful you give me a new way of thinking. Help me to put to death the desires of my old self and to live in the awareness of the new creation you offer me. Thank you for breathing into me the very breath of you which produces love, joy, peace, patience, kindness, goodness, faithfulness, and self-control. Amen.

Worship: "Dead Man Walking" by Jeremy Camp and "Before And After" by Elevation Worship & Maverick City

6

Immanuel—God with Us

The virgin will conceive and give birth to a son, and they will call him Immanuel (which means "God with us").

MATTHEW 1:23

There is major significance about God being "*with us,*" Immanuel! The Bible both begins and ends with the presence of God *with us.* In the book of Genesis, God is shown walking through the Garden of Eden, having conversations with Adam and Eve as if it's just another casual "day in the life" (Genesis 3:8). Fast forward to the end of the Bible as John is given a future glimpse of the "end times" on earth and we are transitioned into a new world. Here again, we see God physically dwelling *with us,* the people he delights in and loves so much, "wiping every tear from our eyes," taking away our heartache and pain (Revelation 21:1-4). That is the beginning and the end of the story. For now, we find ourselves somewhere in the middle, sandwiched between both those times when God is physically present with us. Though it feels sometimes as if we've been left completely alone, this is not the truth. Though we're living between the "Once upon a time...," and the "...happily ever after," we are still able to enjoy intimacy with Almighty God.

How is this possible? Two thousand years ago, Jesus entered planet earth and changed life as we had known. Immanuel! It was such a significant moment—our calendars are forever dated—our lives forever changed. God the Son came to earth, to be *with us*—Immanuel!

Jesus walked among us, experiencing the sufferings of humanity and a painful death that we may know an even deeper experience of Immanuel (God with us). Although his physical body left earth, God now walks with us in another form. If we allow him in, his presence—the Spirit—takes up residence in our hearts.

Consider Christmastime. For many of us, this season offered us happy experiences and joyful memories when we were children, but through the years in the wake of loss and rejection, it became the hardest time of year. Christmastime, more than any other time of year, puts our loneliness at the front and center. Ironically, healing for our loneliness comes when we recall the essential message of Christmas—the gift we've been given, Immanuel, has come and God is indeed still *with us.* Settle in and bask in the knowledge that the one who most loves our souls is here! Immanuel, God's Sprit with us, is about undoing loneliness.

Oftentimes, it is during our most difficult times God feels most distant. Knowing God means we are aware of his presence and, at other times, perceive his absence. Sometimes we lose the *perception* of his nearness because we have built a wall around our hearts to endure the pain of life. Sometimes, we simply shut him out with noise, busyness, and forgetfulness. Dietrich Bonhoeffer, in his book, *Temptation,* said, "Satan does not here fill us with hatred of God, but with forgetfulness of God."[1]

During these times of perceived distance, we must remember God Immanuel, open our closed and grieving hearts, be intentional about silence and solitude, and bask in his presence. Then will our hearts notice God there, pursuing us, leaving us whispers of his love. The more room we make to acknowledge his presence, the more we will experience his presence. We must clear the clutter in our busy schedules. We must make a space in our hearts for him. We must take the time to be aware and listen because it comes in a gentle whisper (1 Kings 19:11-12).

If you are feeling alone, make space in your schedule, a regular meeting time and place, and ask God to meet you there. What do you need right now—perhaps strength, peace, joy, hope, fully understood, and loved? He's got all of it and he longs to fill your needs. Lay your soul at his feet in prayer, listen to worship, read from his Word, reflect on his truth, write down that truth, soak in his love, pursue intimacy with him. Come into this time fully anticipating that he will renew his presence in your life. Look for him throughout the day. He is with us, God Immanuel!

Reflection: Recall a time when you undeniably felt God's presence. How did you know it was him? When have you felt his absence? Isn't it ironic that the time of year we celebrate God Immanuel is the time we often lose sight of his presence in our busyness? How can we remember God with us throughout busy seasons? Decide to make a physical space and dedicate a specific time, even if it means getting up earlier or going to bed a little later, every day this week to experience Immanuel. To ensure it happens, ask someone to hold you accountable. Tell them when and where this meeting will take place and ask them to check on you. At the end of the week, share with your accountability partner what happened between you and God during this time.

Prayer: God, I appreciate that you want to be with me. It's so easy to clutter my life with things that hide you from my mind. I pray you would help me keep regular "dates" with you to experience your presence in my life. I come into these meetings fully anticipating your presence. I look forward to learning something new and drawing closer to you. Amen

---

Worship: "Never Once" by One Sonic Society and "In The Middle" by Jonathan David & Melissa Helser

7

We Are Not Alone

And I will ask the Father, and he will give you another advocate to help you and be with you forever— the Spirit of truth. The world cannot accept him, because it neither sees him nor knows him. But you know him, for he lives with you and will be in you. I will not leave you as orphans; I will come to you.

John 14:16-18

I've often wondered what it would have been like to spend time in the company of Jesus when he walked the earth. He was here for such a short time, then he left saying he was going to prepare a place for us in Heaven. Jesus's friends and followers were dismayed to learn he was leaving. Imagine their feelings of confusion and distress. We can conclude their feelings were of desperation as Jesus compared their loss to that of orphans. But he assured them that though he was leaving, God's presence would continue to be with them. This presence of God differs from Jesus in that we aren't able to see him, touch him, or audibly hear him. However, he is in another way the same as Jesus.

In Genesis 1:26, God refers to himself in the plural form. He says, "Let us make mankind in our image, in our likeness..." God refers to himself as "us" and "our." To whom is God referring? The answer is Jesus (John 1:1-3, 14) and the Spirit (Genesis 1:2).

Jesus said he would send *another* advocate, or helper. In the Greek, there are two words for *another*. One is *allos*, which means it is exactly the same kind—same character. The other is *heteros*, which refers to a different kind. Here, John uses the former, indicating the Spirit sent in his place is of the same character as Jesus. The Spirit of God within *us* is of the same character as Jesus!

God knew all we'd face in this world—the challenges, the heartache, the brokenness, and the mind-blowing confusion of our broken world. He knew, in our finite strength alone, we could not possibly navigate the mountains, the valleys, the roadblocks and the rapids that threaten to sweep us away. With all knowledge of what's ahead, he, God the Spirit, guides us with perfect wisdom. The Holy Spirit walks with us through this corrupt and broken world. He is described as our Advocate (NIV), Helper (NKJV & ESV) or Comforter (KJV) (John 14:26).

His presence resides in those who have accepted Jesus. Those with this Spirit learn his voice, his tug, and the effect he has on their lives. To those with the Spirit, he is a certainty. But Jesus said, "The world cannot accept him, because it neither sees him nor knows him. But you know him, for he lives with you and will be in you" (John 14:17). The world cannot understand him. For those who've never experienced him, simply the idea of him sounds ludicrous.

If you are among those whom Jesus says "cannot accept him" because you don't see or know him, yes, you can experience the comfort, encouragement, correction, wisdom, and direction he offers. If you want this Advocate, he's yours. I encourage you to take a leap of faith and ask that you would come to see him and know him.

You only need to accept Jesus as your Savior and the Holy Spirit will then make his entrance into your heart. Just as Jesus does not force his way to give comfort or healing to those who don't want it ("Do you want to be healed?" John 5:6 ESV), the Holy Spirit is of the same character. We must invite him in. We must take the responsibility in receiving this Advocate. We must open ourselves up and plant the Word in our hearts so the Holy Spirit can remind us of the promises. We must surrender our minds to be transformed. We must set aside our own desires and make room for a truth that might—no, will—conflict with our own.

Reflection: What are your thoughts about the Spirit? Have you invited God/Jesus/Spirit into your life? If you have not yet, consider taking this step of faith. (A prayer below is provided if you want help verbalizing the invitation.) If you have taken this step of faith, can you think of a time when you unmistakably felt the presence and work of the Holy Spirit directing, counseling, or comforting you through a situation?

Prayer: God, I know I need you. I know I'm a sinner and the sin in my life has separated me from you. I'm in need of forgiveness. I'm in need of an Advocate to get to you. Jesus, I ask you to reach across the canyon created by my own sin. Spirit of God, I ask you to move into my heart so I may have the comfort, guidance, and counsel of your perfect wisdom. I accept the life you have been waiting to give me—the life of abundance. I know you never promised the road with you would be easy but I'm holding on to the promise that you are holding me as we walk it together. Help me to come to know your Spirit—your voice. I pray I would not shut out the gentle whisper of your voice but learn to sense it in all circumstances. Amen.

Worship: "Walk With Me" by Jesus Culture, "Holy Ghost" by Maverick City Music, and "Come Holy Spirit" by Vertical Worship

8

Roles of the Spirit

And I will ask the Father, and he will give you another advocate to help you and be with you forever— the Spirit of truth. The world cannot accept him, because it neither sees him nor knows him. But you know him, for he lives with you and will be in you. I will not leave you as orphans; I will come to you.

John 14:16-18

Many are acquainted with the work and ministry of Jesus but are not as familiar with the work and ministry of the Holy Spirit. The Spirit plays many roles in our lives. He is amazing, having polar attributes—powerful enough to create a universe and take down a king, yet quiet and gentle as a whisper or a simple nudge in our hearts.

He guides us by closing certain doors leading to harm (Acts 16:6-7) and opens new doors (Acts 10:19-20). He teaches and reminds us what we have learned (John 14:26). (We are oh-so-forgetful!) He translates the groans of our hearts to the Father. There are times when life gets too difficult, and in our overwhelmed state of desperation, our souls attempt to utter a cry to God but spoken words are beyond reach. Those times when our brokenness runs so deep there is no language, all we can utter is, "Dear God...," before the tears flood and we are left speechless. The Spirit brings our groans to Heaven in precise descriptions of our pain and clear requests for help, translating our lament to God (Romans 8:26).

He is the still, small voice of God in times of pain. When we are surrounded by hate, he reminds us who we are and that we are loved (Romans 5:5). When we face doubt, he increases our faith (Ephesians 3:16-17). When we are dealt cynicism, he points out the good. When we're feeling despair, he fills us with hope. When we're in the midst of contention and battles, he gives us peace

(Romans 15:13). When we are fed lies, he shows us the truth (John 14:26). When we are confused, he brings wisdom and clarity into our minds at just the right time (Ephesians 1:17).

It's difficult to sum up this Spirit. Various English translations of the Bible call him "Helper" (ESV), "Advocate" (NIV), and "Comforter" (KJV), and rightly so. As I study him deeper, what comes to mind over and over is *he is FOR me.* And he is FOR YOU!

Reflection: Knowing the Spirit speaks in gentle whispers, how can you ensure you will not miss his voice? In what ways can you lean on him? In what areas can you surrender to his work in your life? Take some steps this week toward quietly listening as the Spirit reminds and guides you.

Prayer: Holy Spirit, thank you for being with me, inside me, and FOR me! Help me to come to know more fully the ways you help me, advocate for me, and comfort me. May I learn to sense your presence, to recognize your voice, to tune in, and to lean on your guidance. Help me to know when you say "go," and when you would have me stop and back up. Help me to embrace the truth you speak to me about who I am and who you are. Amen.

Worship: "Spirit Speak" by Austin French and "Spirit of God" by Planetshakers

9

The Deceit of the Heart

The heart is deceitful above all things and beyond cure. Who can understand it?

JEREMIAH 17:9

Some believe we humans are innately "good" at the core of our being. I think we can all take a look at a two-year-old and see that our innate selves are not "good." At our core, we are selfish, jealous, demanding, and complain about everything. The heart, in its deceit, blinds us to our true corruption and disguises itself to look good—even admirable. We are tricked into believing we are good in our core, we don't need to change, and we don't need a Savior.

However, we can't trust our hearts. Some people do trust their heart, making it their god, following where it leads, going with whatever *feels right* in the moment. The problem with this line of thinking is there can only be one truth. Truth can only be discovered, not created by a sensation. There is no "your truth" and "my truth." It only stands to reason that if there is a "your truth" and a "my truth," and they are opposing, one is not the truth. There is only THE truth.

"Follow your heart," our culture says, "It will lead you to happiness." Lie. "It will lead you home." Lie. "It is always right." Lie. Proverbs 3:5 tells us not to lean on our own understanding [not to follow our hearts]. Are we able to look down on creation and see the big picture with the past, the future, and everyone's puzzle piece as part of the whole? No, we are limited in our knowledge, which skews our perceptions about what is good and what is in our best interest. But God sees and knows all. Proverbs 3 goes on to say in verse 6, "In all your ways submit to him, and he will make your paths straight." It's saying to *not* follow your heart, but instead to trust God who sees your rugged and twisted path and knows how to straighten it out.

Our hearts lie to us because we don't want to realize the significance of our sin. Instead of recognizing our sin as being traitorous to God, deserving of death, we believe it's worthy of little more than a slap on the hand or a kind little shake of God's head. And so, our hearts deceive us to protect our egos.

We can easily see the flaws in someone else, but our own flaws are not as apparent to us. Even when we think we want to know when we're in the wrong, our protective defenses justify and minimize our errors. We tend to make excuses for our behavior, brush it off like it's no big deal. But guess what—it's a big deal to God! He sees not only our actions, but the *root* of our actions—the thought that launched us into sin, detestable to God. He knows whether our actions are sincere or hiding behind selfish motives, whether we're honest in our hearts or hypocritical, whether we're flattering someone to gain something or if we're genuinely intending the praise we give.

Even David, the man after God's own heart, knew his own heart was deceitful. He knew he *needed* to chase after God's heart. He wrote, "Search me, God, know my heart; test me and know my anxious thoughts. See if there is any offensive way in me, and lead me in the way everlasting" (Psalm 139:23-24). David was asking God to show him his sin because he wanted, more than anything, to be lead in God's ways. Only when we are aligning our hearts with God's can we be sure we're not being led down a path of deception.

Studying the truth of Scripture is important so we can use it to align our hearts. We should examine our hearts regularly and ask, *Am I following my heart? Or am I following the solid rock of unchanging truth?* Sometimes examination uncovers things we don't want to address. Let's take the high road, though it be the difficult road, and seek truth no matter our heart's desire.

Reflection: How has your heart deceived you in the past? How are you currently following the way of your heart? Does that way align with the truth of Scripture? How is your heart currently deceiving you (desires that go against what you know to be true)? How is the state of your heart while you're at your job? While dealing with your kids? With extended family? With your spouse?

Prayer: Almighty God, I know only you see the entire picture, every situation, and all the answers. I also know my insight is limited, so I depend on you to go ahead of me and straighten my paths. I pray I would not lean on my own deceitful heart, but instead on your ways. Amen.

Worship: "Dear Heart" by Sanctus Real, "Blind" by Third Day, and "Captain" by Hillsong UNITED

10

The Conduct Reward

I the L*ORD search the heart and examine the mind, to reward each person according to their conduct, according to what their deeds deserve.*

JEREMIAH 17:10

Talented athletes are rewarded with trophies. Hard-working students receive good grades and scholarships. Rewards on the job often consist of a raise or a paid commission. In life, we work hard, we get a prize. And so it is with God! He rewards us according to our deeds and conduct.

Some might picture our deeds weighed on a scale with our good deeds on one side and our bad deeds on the other, with the "heaviest" deeds deciding the fate of our afterlife. That's not a thing. Nothing we *do* earns us the prize of Heaven. Eternal life is not earned as a reward; it's a gift. Accepting Jesus as the Savior of our lives grants us the gates of Heaven. As far as determining our fate, it really is that simple (Ephesians 2:8-9).

However, our deeds here on earth are *rewarded* diversely in the afterlife. 1 Corinthians 15:41-42 says, "The sun has one kind of splendor, the moon another and the stars another; and star differs from star in splendor. So will it be with the resurrection of the dead." Just as stars differ in splendor, so will we in Heaven. Think of our good deeds as seeds that plant into our eternities. When our time in this world is done, the good-deed-seeds we planted sprout into something splendid in Heaven. Consider eternity is a long time. Do we really want to just "slide" into Heaven, displaying the lowest rank of splendor for our eternities? Or do we want to shine with optimum splendor forever?

Though our good deeds don't save us, God expects them from us and, in fact, has prepared good works in advance for us to do (Ephesians 2:10). Not only will he reward us in Heaven for them, he will reward us here on earth as well. A few examples: Love and faithfulness earn us a good name (Proverbs 3:3-4). Obedience brings us both joy and a prosperous life (Deuteronomy 5:33, John 15:10-11). Prayer and thanksgiving give us peace (Philippians 4:6-7). Humility earns riches, honor, and life (Proverbs 22:4). Giving generously to others is rewarded, in turn, with our own provision (Luke 6:38). When we follow God's plan, we are rewarded. Likewise, when we step outside the will of God, we miss so much he had in store for us.

Interestingly, it's our hearts and minds that are examined to determine our reward. Offering a gift with a hidden, selfish motive isn't going to cut it. God is more interested in the thoughts, motives, and intentions that prompted our actions. Start planting the good-deed-seeds, but as you do, check yourself for pure motives. May we be able to say with David, "Search me, God, know my heart; test me and know my anxious thoughts. See if there is any offensive way in me, and lead me in the way everlasting."

Reflection: Consider the fact that God prepared works in advance for you to complete. What works do you think he has prepared for you? How would your actions change in light of knowing God searches your heart and mind to determine the reward for your deeds?

Prayer: Dear God, I pray you would give me opportunities to plant good deeds and clearly direct me to the works you prepared for me to do. Please give me the time, energy, motivation, organization, and ideas to get them done well. I pray as you search my heart and mind, you would only find pure, sincere motives. I look forward to eternity with you and the rewards you have in store for me. Thank you. Amen.

Worship: "Headed For The Mountain" by Micah Tyler and "Create In Me" by Rend Collective

11

Forgive Others

Make allowance for each other's faults, and forgive anyone who offends you. Remember, the Lord forgave you, so you must forgive others.

COLOSSIANS 3:13 NLT

Broken people have sharp edges. We have all been broken to some extent, therefore, we all have shards like little glass daggers pointing outward, ready to jab others. Even if we go about our day trying to keep our shards from touching others, unintentionally we bump another, hurting them. We so much need the forgiveness of God and others. Fortunately, we have been forgiven by God. Jesus then requires us to extend that forgiveness to others as well. Forgiveness is not simply a suggestion. It is a firm commandment.

"Being resentful, they say, is like taking poison and waiting for the other person to die."[2] Chew on that for a minute. Who suffers when we don't forgive? Possibly the one who wronged us. However, to a deeper extent, *we* decay under the poison of our own unforgiveness. Anger, resentment, and hate become our prisons. And who has control over our prisons? The one who imprisoned us. You and I. We make the decision to either stay in our self-created prison, or to be free, not giving others the control of our emotions.

Many times, we hang onto that grudge because we want our offenders to "pay" for their wrongdoing. This is where we need to *Let go and let God.* The saying is cliché and a little bit cheesy, but it's true! In Deuteronomy 32:35, God says vengeance belongs to him alone. It's not for us to determine one's punishment or execute that punishment. Forgiving another requires complete trust, knowing God will handle it as he promised he would. He not only has our backs, but our best interest in mind. He wants our complete surrender. He wants us to hand over the reins and trust him to handle it his way.

In any healthy relationship, forgiveness is essential. We can't simply chuck every relationship that causes us hurt. We'd be chucking them out right and left. We must operate with forgiveness. No tight family became genuinely close without hard-fought forgiveness. No long-term best friends became chummy without the offering and acceptance of an occasional olive branch. In a marriage, hurt is inevitable. Our marriages will not grow, and may not even survive, without forgiveness. If we want any valuable relationship, forgiveness is essential.

In a relationship where there has been much hurt and we're trying to forgive, move forward, and restore that relationship, it may help us to shift our perspective of the enemy—to view, not the person who wronged us as the enemy, but division as the enemy. To see the wounding action that caused the division—the lie, the snide remark, the cut to the heart—as the true enemy. Families, friends, and spouses must work together to defeat the true enemy, disunity. We do that through forgiveness.

What does forgiveness look like? Does it mean we continue in an abusive relationship, without protective boundaries in place? Absolutely, not. It means we're not going to hold a grudge. We're not going to bring it up again. We're not going to desire hardships for others. Forgiveness means we are going to wish our offenders well. This is hard to do! I have found that praying *for* people helps me let go of my grudge. Praying good things over their life—success in their career, joy in their heart, fulfilling relationships for them. I pray for all the things I want for my own life. I find, after praying *for* them, my heart changes toward them. The shackles of resentment release me from the bondage of anger and bitterness.

In some situations, forgiveness seems impossible, but it is never unattainable with God. We need to pray and ask for the power that's beyond ourselves to forgive. I have read countless stories of courageous people offering forgiveness, such as Corrie ten Boom, Sabina Wurmbrand, and Louis Zamperini. These people were able to forgive horrendous sins against them. God can empower you and me to do the same for those who have wronged us.

When forgiving requires a power beyond the bounds of our capability, it is a powerful way to shine a light in a dark world. When people see our complete surrender of vengeance, they will see God.

Imagine yourself having compassion for someone and doing them a special favor. Now imagine their response is to spit in your face and slap you *while you are completing* this act of kindness. Sickening, right? This is exactly what happened to Jesus. In Matthew 26, we read Jesus surrendered himself to be put on trial for a death that was not deserved. Not by him anyway. It was our death he signed up for. While he was on trial—voluntarily—his face was spat in and took a punch. Even still, he chose the cross for them. For us. His love was unwavering, as should be our love for others. We have this incredible power, the power to do the unthinkable—the power to forgive—within us.

Reflection: Are there any areas of unforgiveness in your life? Consider your extended family, friendships—both past and present, church relationships, marriage, social media interactions, and coworkers. Now shift your focus to the real enemy, disunity. Take the blame off the person and place it on the hurtful words or actions. Release the grip animosity has on you. Pray *for* the person.

Prayer: God, I thank you for offering me forgiveness. I didn't deserve what you did for me. And you didn't deserve my death. Nor did you deserve to be spat on, punched, mocked, lashed, beaten, and hanged. Reveal to me any areas of unforgiveness in my life. Help me to tap into your power within me to forgive them. Though I've been hurt, I won't let it imprison me. [If you feel so led, take time to ask God to bless in specific ways those who have wronged you.] Amen.

Worship: "Where Forgiveness Is" by Sidewalk Prophets and "Forgiven" by Crowder

12

Forget the Past

Forget the former things; do not dwell on the past. See, I am doing a new thing! Now it springs up; do you not perceive it? I am making a way in the wilderness and streams in the wasteland.

Isaiah 43:18-19

When I was diagnosed with an incurable cancer at the age of thirty-five, this passage became my mantra. It gave me the hope I so desperately needed. My good friend had it made into a wall decal for me as a constant reminder that even though my life turned upside-down overnight in a seemingly catastrophic way, God was up to something new! He was going to get me through the wasteland, and in the meantime, was going to miraculously create a new spring of water in that wasteland!

The thought of leaving three young kids behind was heavy and difficult to process. Not only that, my career pursuits were shattered. I had been working for years in college to advance my career. When I was diagnosed with cancer, those hopes, dreams, and pursuits had to be nailed into a coffin. Little did I know at the time of the burial of my hard work and accomplishments that God was up to something good. He put me on a path I never would have traveled by choice prior to diagnosis, and it has indeed been a good place with life-giving streams and springs aplenty.

Both good events and bad events can cause us to linger in the past. If things were good in the past but have taken a turn for the worse, we might be longing for the "good old days" and reminisce about what "used to be." A prior memory might pop up and smack us in the face, causing a tear to escape because things were so much simpler and happier back then. Or it may be that situations of the past were less than ideal and we're feeling "stuck" by thoughts we feel we can't escape. Now, though our circumstances have changed, we're still residing in the hurts of yesterday, still feeling trapped in our own minds due to the trauma that has shaped us. A broken home, past abuse, sins we regret, or a past broken heart, even now, leave us feeling limited and powerless. "Forgetting the former things" and letting go isn't easy, but neither is lugging around baggage that weighs us down emotionally, spiritually, and eventually physically. We may have things that are seared on our hearts, things we can't just "forget" but I believe God is calling us to "forget the former things" as in "do not dwell" there. For some who may have experienced multiple complex trauma, letting go and dwelling in a new place may mean seeking professional help to not "dwell on the past" and to prevent our pain from calling the shots in all our actions and reactions.

Let's learn from Lot's wife. After God told Lot and his wife to flee the wicked city that had been their home, and not look back as that city was being destroyed, Lot's wife looked back at the life she was leaving behind. We can only guess why. It was familiar? She loved the life she built in that place? She lacked trust in God for her future? Lot's wife was unable to "forget the former things" and she paid a high price (Genesis 19:1-26). Are we any different today? We hang on to the "former things" and suffer in the present. Why is it so hard for us? Why do we so often "dwell on the past" and fail to see that he is "doing a new thing," a thing so fresh and full of life? Why do we dwell in the past—regret it, desire for it, or fear a repeat of it—when God is offering something as life-giving as "streams in the wasteland"?

God takes pleasure in providing for us in unexpected ways. "Now to him who is able to do immeasurably more than all we ask or imagine, according to his power that is at work within us," Paul writes in Ephesians 3:20. What he wants for us is *immeasurably more* than what we're asking. His plans are beyond our dreams. They were set for us before we were born, before we were able to dream. He spurs us to victory in new, unexpected ways. He loves to blow our minds. So let go of the past that's holding you back and let God blow your mind.

Reflection: When you get stuck in the past, are you usually reminiscing good times or rehashing bad times? What "good times" do you miss the most? What burden are you carrying from the past? What, from your past, is currently keeping you from moving forward? Are you willing to let it go and allow God to work out for you a better present and future?

Prayer: Father, forgive me for looking back on a past you've asked me to leave behind. I want to let go, but naturally, keep holding on. Thank you for the lesson I learned in my wilderness, but may I now move on, changed. Help me give up what I cannot control and embrace the new that you have placed in front of me. Amen.

Worship: "Walking On Water" by NEEDTOBREATHE and "Living Water" by Ellie Holcomb

13

A New Stream in the Wasteland

Forget the former things; do not dwell on the past See, I am doing a new thing! Now it springs up; do you not perceive it? I am making a way in the wilderness and streams in the wasteland.

Isaiah 43:18-19

Many of us hate change and desire what's familiar, but God wants us stretched until we find ourselves in a "new thing" for that is where we grow. We like control, having tidy little solutions to tidy little problems, and we're not always sure how to handle the "new." Sometimes "new" is terrifying, and our human instinct is to rush back to the familiar. But it could be the past blinding us to the good things right in front of us. We don't easily let go of the reins of our lives. God knows, for most of us, it's only when we get to the end of ourselves that we resort to trusting him. It isn't until we realize we aren't in control anymore that we roll over in surrender. That's when our faith is awakened and we are given a renewed trust in him to discover the impossible "streams in the wasteland."

God is not surprised by our current situations, nor is he aloof regarding our lives. He's intimately invested in us. Instead of presenting our problems to God with an idea of how we think he should fix them, let's take a leap of faith and change our prayers to ask for our eyes and hearts to be open to the new that he is doing.

Notice God's description of what "new" is. It's not an escape plan that spawned out of our limited abilities or short-sighted perspectives. "New" is the impossible, unexpected things he does. Roadways in the wilderness? Rivers in the wasteland? (Some versions, ESV and KJV, use the word *desert.*) These are not the natural things we expect! But for us to discover that roadway in the wilderness, we first must face our inability to work out a solution on our own. When we focus on him and trust his new ways, he makes a way for beauty to flow back into our circumstances. Notice he does not say, "I'm making a way *out* of the wilderness," or "I'm making a way to *material prosperity.*" He says he is making a way in the wasteland—in the midst of pain, in the midst of loss—and it will be as refreshing as is a drink for one dying of thirst.

"Do you not perceive it?" God asks. He knows we often don't see what's right in front of us or trust it will come. Ask God to help you have faith to perceive it, to have the slightest glimpse of that path through your wilderness. Then dwell there, in expectation, for the streams in the wasteland that are about to quench your thirst.

Reflection: Can you think of a time in the past when God made a way through your wilderness, but you didn't perceive it until after you were rescued? What impossible situation are you currently facing? How can you look at this impossible situation in a different light to perceive and trust that God is doing something new?

Prayer: God, our Rescuer, thank you for new paths and rivers in my impossible situations. Help me to perceive your presence, your hand in my troubles. Show me a glimpse of what you're doing. Help me to trust it's all good and to fix my eyes forward in anticipation. I'm ready for you to blow my mind. Amen.

Worship: "Know You Will" by Hillsong UNITED and "God You Are Good" by Citizen Way

14

How Wide, Long, High, and Deep

And I pray that you, being rooted and established in love, may have power, together with all the Lord's holy people, to grasp how wide and long and high and deep is the love of Christ, and to know this love that surpasses knowledge—that you may be filled to the measure of all the fullness of God.

Ephesians 3:17-19

We've all been told, "Jesus loves you." But many of us have failed to grasp the enormity and intensity of that love. Comprehending the extent of it is beyond the reach of the human heart and mind alone. Just how great is Christ's love for us? Paul says it's too great to know on our own, that we need "power" to grasp it. He says, not individually, but "together with all the Lord's holy people," is an important component. Not only that, but we need "roots" in love to grasp this great love for us. That's a complex love. We're going to dive into each section of this verse to gain one more crumb of an understanding of God's love.

Paul described Christ's love as "wide and long and high and deep." There are multiple theories about what Paul meant by this. For example, the directions of the cross—pointing across and up and down. Some believe the dimensions compare the church to the Temple specifications. We can't be sure Paul intended these analogies. We can, however, be sure he meant God's love is great, beyond measure. It is interesting, though, to think about just *how infinite* is the reach of God's love.

God's love is wide. His love extends to every nation, race, and gender. Jews, Gentiles, and every nation. Men, women, and children. It doesn't matter what you believe, how you feel, how you were raised, what you've done in the past. God is love. And he loves *you.*

God's love is long. It is the length of eternity, reaching from the first living beings, through the ages, to today and beyond into eternity. You were loved when you made the biggest mistake of your life. You are loved right here in this present moment. And his love will be where you are tomorrow. You never have to go one day without God's love.

God's love is high. In fact, God is called "Most High" all throughout Scripture. His love is as high as the heavens. He raises us high, above our enemies (2 Samuel 22:49 & Psalm 18:48). His love reaches down to us and then lifts us high to share his throne in Heaven (Revelation 3:21). This is the height of God's love.

God's love is deep. Though God is on high, and humanity has fallen, we haven't fallen past the reach of God's love. His love reaches down through the vastness of the universe and covers our sin. There is no pit of sin too deep for God's love to reach into and pull us out upon our first call to him (Psalm 71:20).

Our human capacity to love can only reach so far. We love more deeply those whom we know more fully than those who are only acquaintances. The intensity of our love varies depending on our knowledge of others. In the same way, our love for God can only go as far as our knowledge of him. But God's knowledge of us is infinite, just as is his love for us.

Think about that for a minute. God knows you and he loves you deeply. There is a place in his heart for you and he rejoices over you (Zephaniah 3:17). Christ's love for you is so immense! Go wide, go long. Search high and deep. You will never find the end of his great love.

Reflection: Recall a few sins you've committed. Envision God's love covering those sins. When was the last time you felt unlovable? Contemplate the truth of God's love for you even then. Take a moment to close your eyes and visualize God lifting you from the pit of your sin, but then he doesn't just lift you out of the pit and set you down outside of it. He keeps lifting you higher and higher until you are seated with him on his throne.

Prayer: Most High God, you are the lover of my soul. No one loves me to the extent you do. Though my sin is deep, and you hate it so much, I'm grateful for your love which reaches deep enough to pull me out. Thank you for lifting me to the heights with you, though I'm not equal to you and I don't deserve it. I can never thank you enough. I pray I would live in the knowledge of your love for me. Amen.

Worship: "Wide, High, Long, Deep" by Ellie Holcomb and "Lifter" by Housefires

15

The Love of Christ to Be Grasped

And I pray that you, being rooted and established in love, may have power, together with all the Lord's holy people, to grasp how wide and long and high and deep is the love of Christ, and to know this love that surpasses knowledge—that you may be filled to the measure of all the fullness of God.

Ephesians 3:17-19

If we think God loves us because we are so loveable, then we haven't fully comprehended the love of Christ. Until we understand just how much God hates the sin in our lives and just how ineligible we are for his love, we can't fully understand it (Psalm 5:4-6). Sin induces God's anger (John 3:36). He cannot tolerate it (Habakkuk 1:13). Since we have sin in our lives, we are loved *not* because we are worthy, but because of the truth of who God is. God is love. Despite his severe disdain for our sin, despite how unworthy we are, Christ continues to love us. Only when we understand this truth can we begin to grasp the depth of his love.

Have you ever been in a relationship with someone who drew you in with his or her kindness and affection, but at other times, pushed you away with lies and disrespect? We know these are toxic relationships. Yet, we all are guilty of dishing out this type of behavior to God. We commit ourselves to him but as soon as something goes wrong, we are shaking our fists at him and questioning his love for us. Our love for him is wavering. I can't tell you how many times things in my life went "wrong" and I questioned God's goodness, only to find he had plans to bring it all together for my good. Though we run hot and cold, God's love toward us remains faithful.

Before we go hanging our heads in shame, thinking we are of no value due to our sin and fluctuating faith, let's remember something—how much we cost. The worth of anything is established by its cost. Our cost? The life of Jesus, paid with painstaking agony. To him, we were worth that price.

While other religions are concerned with humanity's pursuit of God, Christianity is about God's pursuit of us. God desires us and pursues us. When we fully understand Christ's love for us, it's a game-changer. It changes our view of "self," our perspective of the world, our priorities, and the way we love others.

Reflection: What was the most toxic relationship you were involved in? Are their similarities between the way you were treated in that relationship and the way you have treated God? Even though you have been less-than-steadfast, can you see God's consistent pursuit of you? How has he shown his goodness and love in your life?

Prayer: Merciful Father, I know I am loved, not because I am worthy, but because you are good. Forgive me for questioning your goodness. Thank you for your faithfulness and constant pursuit of me. Help me to remember the undeserved love you give me as I consider how to respond to others. May I be more like you and offer mercy and unconditional love to others. Amen.

Worship: "Still You Love Me" by Aaron Shust and "Mystery Of Mercy" by Caedmon's Call

16

To Know This Love That Surpasses Knowledge

And I pray that you, being rooted and established in love, may have power, together with all the Lord's holy people, to grasp how wide and long and high and deep is the love of Christ, and to know this love that surpasses knowledge—that you may be filled to the measure of all the fullness of God.

EPHESIANS 3:17-19

We are to "know" this love that "surpasses knowledge." How can we know something that's impossible to be known? It takes a miracle. And so, Paul prays for the power of the Holy Spirit to work God's love into the depths of our hearts, minds, and souls.

The Greek word for *know* in this text is *ginosko*, which is not the gaining of book-knowledge but the gaining of knowledge through experience. Feelings can't be taught. We can only know about feelings by experiencing them. Similarly, to know God's love, we must experience it, personally. Simply reading about God's love won't help us to "know this love that surpasses knowledge." Reading about God's love in the Bible and hearing stories of Jesus's love for people—ordinary and sinful people like us—is a great place to begin to learn the depths of his love. But the full experience of God's love comes through intentional intimacy and prayer. Psalm 34:8 tells us, "Taste and see that the LORD is good…" We first "taste" God's goodness and then we can "see." First comes the experience, then comes the understanding, the knowing.

We do not know what it is like to be full of glory, to be all-powerful, to create an entire universe, only to be rejected by our creation. We do not know what it is like to empty oneself of all this power and glory to walk among people we deeply love, only to watch them tread on that love with indifference. We do not know what it was like to take on all the sin of the world throughout all time—yours, mine, and everyone—through the past and in the future. We do not know what Jesus felt as he screamed, "My God, my God, why have you forsaken me?" (Matthew 27:46). We do not know what agonizing death is like. Therefore, we *cannot* grasp the depth of Christ's love toward us.

We cannot grasp Christ's love for us through book-knowledge alone. We can read about Christ's love for us in the Bible. We can listen to the preachers tell us, "Jesus loves you." We can listen to podcasts about his love all day long. But if we can't move that knowledge from our heads to our hearts, we cannot grasp his love. Until we have experienced his love in our own lives, we will not "know" that which surpasses knowledge.

In any relationship, falling in love is easy. Sustaining that love is the hard part. We must continuously put effort toward the relationship if we want it to grow. In the same way, if we aren't constantly growing in our knowledge of God and our experience with God, we are missing the wonder, the mystery of a love so remarkable Paul calls it "surpassing" love.

How can you experience God's love? First, prayer is key. Ask God to help you experience it. Then be intentional about pursuing knowledge through experiences with God. Shut out negative thoughts in your head. The enemy commonly lies, whispering: *You are not good enough. You have to be perfect for God to love you. You will never overcome your struggles. You are alone.*

You can't experience God's love when you're listening to the enemy. When good things come to you, give the credit to God, the giver of all good and perfect things. When bad things happen, don't blame God, but trust he has a plan and will make beauty from the ashes. Keep your eyes open and look for the ways he comes through. When God asks you to do something risky, take those steps in faith and watch the good unfold. Write any experiences you have in a journal to remember.

Christ's love is not merely for the book-smart people. Jesus prayed in Matthew 11:25, "I praise you, Father, Lord of heaven and earth, because you have hidden these things from the wise and learned, and revealed them to little children." God's love is open for anyone with a heart and willingness to learn from experience. It is open for you. Invest. Learn. Experience. Grow deeper in love.

Reflection: What is something you didn't think you would love when you first heard of it, but after experiencing it, you couldn't help but love?

When have you experienced God's love? How can you move the book-knowledge of Jesus's love to your own life experiences? Choose at least one of the above-mentioned ways you will work on starting today.

Prayer: Loving God, the depth of your love is so difficult to grasp. I pray for supernatural power to know it. I pray for experiences to help me know without a shadow of a doubt that you love me. Amen.

Worship: "If We Only Knew" by Unspoken and "All In My Head" by Seven Places

17

Rooted and Established in Love

And I pray that you, being rooted and established in love, may have power, together with all the Lord's holy people, to grasp how wide and long and high and deep is the love of Christ, and to know this love that surpasses knowledge—that you may be filled to the measure of all the fullness of God.

EPHESIANS 3:17-19

Some childhoods are filled with anger and neglect. From the day some are born, they learn they are nothing more than an inconvenience. For people who know nothing through experiencing love from those they can touch and see, how are they to know the love of the one they cannot touch and see? We can't let our experience with *people* define *God's* love.

Paul says we are to be "rooted and established in love." Roots burrow through the dirt and absorb nutrients, giving life to the tree. What we immerse ourselves in is what feeds or kills our souls. If we plunge our roots down into others' opinions of our self-worth, we will never measure up. We will never feel loved enough, wanted enough, and satisfied. When we run to imperfect people, incapable of loving perfectly, to seek love that satisfies completely, we put more pressure on them than they can handle. No one has the ability to love as deeply as we want to be loved. People's love will *always* lead to disappointment. Only God's love is wide and long and high and deep enough to love us perfectly and satisfy our souls. Burrow into that!

If we plunge our roots down into the solid, unshakeable love of Christ, we will flourish. When times of drought come into our lives and the love and acceptance of other people are nowhere to be found, we continue to thrive because we are rooted and established in the endless supply of Christ's love. Being rooted in Christ's love means we make it our mission, our purpose in life, to learn about this love and to marinate in it. It becomes the center of everything we do, so much so, that others' opinions of us don't affect our self-worth. We're not knocked off our feet when we're left out, misunderstood, or mistreated. When we're rooted in Christ, we don't need to be validated by others. We don't need to put on a show to prove to others we are smart, funny, cool, or whatever performance we think will prove our worth. Christ's love tells us everything we need to know about ourselves.

My friend's husband called her ugly. Her response to him? "I am beautiful because I'm a child of God." This is the truth. I think, however, most of us, myself included, would allow that criticism to grow and entwine itself around us until we have choked on it. We would feel defeat. We wouldn't stand up to the accusations of the enemy but would allow it to sink us. This woman's roots were established deep in Christ's love.

God is pursuing you with that same love. The next time the enemy speaks lies to you, whether in your head or through another person, stand up to his lies. Tell the liar to back off! Remind yourself, "I am a Child of God, deeply loved by the King."

Reflection: How often are your thoughts on how to please people in order to feel loved? How much does it affect you when others are cruel or rude to you? How much are your thoughts based on God's love for you? How can you remind yourself, at times when you feel defeated by others, that you are loved by the Father just as you are?

Prayer: God of Love, sometimes I let other people's opinions affect my self-worth. I don't want to let others define me. Thank you for defining me as your child, wanted and worthy of dying for. Thank you for filling my need for love and acceptance, no matter the circumstances in my life. I pray I wouldn't find a need to dig my roots elsewhere. I pray my roots would plunge deep into your love only. I pray as I spend time indulging in your truths about me, I would be satisfied. Amen.

Worship: "You Say" by Lauren Daigle, "Wanted" by Danny Gokey and "Unstoppable Love" by Jesus Culture

18

Together With All the Lord's Holy People

And I pray that you, being rooted and established in love, may have power, together with all the Lord's holy people, to grasp how wide and long and high and deep is the love of Christ, and to know this love that surpasses knowledge—that you may be filled to the measure of all the fullness of God.

EPHESIANS 3:17-19

Sean had seen God's hand in his own life. It was a few years back and that started his journey of faith. But he hadn't seen God's hand moving recently. Doubts about God's existence began creeping into the corners of his mind. While listening to a podcast, Sean felt prompted to get plugged in with other believers from church. After meeting with these believers, Sean was enlightened. He met Ryan who shared about having been diagnosed with cancer that had spread throughout his body. After being prayed over, Ryan went in for a PET scan only to discover no cancer anywhere in his body. Maggie shared that though she also prayed for healing from cancer, she wasn't given healing but was given increased faith and peace and a clear vision of God's hand in her life. Through it all, her grandson gave his life to Jesus, which gave her more joy than any physical healing would have given her. Bob shared about his alcohol addiction, how he had tried everything, but was unable to sober up until he met Jesus and never turned back. Katie shared about how God helped her overcome low self-worth. Seeking value, she had turned to men and endured a succession of abusive relationships, but God showed her how valuable she truly is and led her into a healthy marriage. Listening to the stories of others and the way God was working in their lives encouraged Sean. He could see God was still on the move.

Having a personal relationship with God is vitally important. However, a personal relationship with God that isn't shared with other believers greatly limits our perspective of God's love and power. God may be doing some great things in your life at this present time. But we all go through periods of time when we're not seeing God's hand as evidently as we are at other times. As God reveals himself in various ways to each person, it is only through a combined experience we can have a greater understanding of who God is, how he works, and how great is his love for us. "Together, with all the Lord's holy people" is where we find the power to grasp how wide, long, high, and deep is Christ's love. We were never meant to experience God in isolation. It takes the body of Christ to experience God wholly.

Our topic verse interestingly uses the word "holy" to describe the people who will have this power to grasp Christ's love. Why is this? Sin blinds us. When we have sin in our lives, though we may not feel blinded, the wool has certainly been pulled over our eyes. "Blessed are the pure in heart, for they will see God" (Matthew 5:8). "For the LORD is righteous, he loves justice; the upright will see his face" (Psalm 11:7). "Surely God is good to Israel, to those who are pure in heart" (Psalm 73:1). We know God loves all people, but these verses indicate that the ability to see God's love and goodness follows purity in heart.

We can't win God's love by being good. Nor can we lose it by being bad. But we can become blind to his love because of our sin. If we're not feeling God's love in our lives, we must examine ourselves for an action or attitude blinding us from the reality of God's love.

To feel Christ's love more evidently, get connected with other believers and get rid of the sin in your life. It is then, "together with all the Lord's holy people," you will have the power to grasp this love that surpasses knowledge.

Reflection: Think of three people whose testimonies have inspired your own faith. If you're not connected with other believers, what steps do you need to take to get plugged in? Is there any sin in your life that could be clouding your vision of God?

Prayer: Father, thank you for your love which is wide, long, high, and deep. Please reveal any sin in my life which may be blinding me to that love. I pray you would guide me to other believers. I pray for opportunities to hear other people's stories of faith. Please reveal yourself to me more completely. May my faith be strengthened through the testimonies of others. Give me the boldness to share with others how you have worked in my life and I pray I would be an encouragement to them as well. Amen.

Worship: "The Purest Place" by Watermark and "We Will Stand" by Carola

19

That You May Be Filled to the Measure of All the Fullness of God

And I pray that you, being rooted and established in love, may have power, together with all the Lord's holy people, to grasp how wide and long and high and deep is the love of Christ, and to know this love that surpasses knowledge—that you may be filled to the measure of all the fullness of God.

EPHESIANS 3:17-19

When we come to "know this love" of Christ, we are filled with the fullness of God. We can be filled with sorrow, filled with joy, filled with anger, or filled with pride. When we are filled with something, the attribute that fills us influences our behavior. When we are filled with the fullness of God, then no matter our circumstances, it is God who influences our actions.

Saturated by God, we see the bigger picture—the Kingdom picture. We are different from others in many ways. We know the value of others and love them as he does. When the world sees someone as inferior, we see beautiful because we have his eyesight. We care for others and are moved to serve them. We aren't motivated by fear, but by faith. We don't act on our human emotion but consider God's greater plan as we go in the direction he leads. We are in tune with where he is moving. We listen for his voice and obey even when he guides us down a road we don't want to go. We strive for holiness. We choose the virtuous but difficult road. Being filled with God means we are like God and reflect his image to others (Ephesians 4:24, 1 Corinthians 15:49).

Just as we can't pour water into a cup already full, we can't be filled with God when we're full of "self." We must empty ourselves of "self" to make room for the fullness of God. Emptying "self" means getting rid of pride, self-promotion, self-reliance, greed, self-righteousness, the need to impress others, envy, attention-seeking behavior, and self-gratification. We know we have emptied ourselves when we can say with conviction, *God, apart from you, I am nothing. Only you can satisfy.* It is at this point, we can begin being filled with God, and the yearnings for other things fade away until we have reached the fullness of God.

Emptying self and filling with God isn't automatic. When we commit our lives to Christ, our selfish desires don't just disappear into thin air. We may or may not "feel" his love. Feelings come and go. Problems come our way and our natural tendencies rear their ugly heads. It's a daily battle of dying to "self" and filling with God's love. When "self" tries to pop up like a jack-in-the-box, we must toss him out again and make the time to refill on God's love.

How much time do we spend thinking about our to-do list, worrying about all the "what-ifs," hashing out solutions to our predicaments and losing focus? How much time do we spend marinating in Christ's love for us, letting it soak into our souls, allowing it to reform our perspectives? That self-evaluation exposes my heart and disproportionate thoughts. My focus is too much on my problems and not enough on Christ's love.

Not realizing Christ's love is the dilemma of humanity. Allow yourself to be immersed in Christ's love. Allow that to capture and move you into the greater picture, the movement of the Kingdom.

Reflection: Think of a time your actions were opposed to your natural desires and you knew that was due to God filling you. What part of your "self" keeps popping up its ugly head—pride, self-promotion, self-reliance, greed, self-righteousness, the need to impress others, envy, attention-seeking behavior, or self-gratification? Can you think of another selfish characteristic with which you struggle? Consider ways to incorporate God's love for you into your daily thoughts.

Prayer: God of Love, when I'm surrounded by my busyness and problems and my natural tendencies keep popping up, it's easy for me to lose sight of your love and purpose for me. Empty me of all my ugly and selfish ways. Fill me with only you until you are the only thing I long for. May others see your love in me and desire it for themselves. Thank you for your constant supply of love. Amen.

Worship: "Let Yourself Be Loved" by MercyMe, "Christ In Me" by Jeremy Camp, and "Keep Making Me" by Sidewalk Prophets

20

The Leash of Fear

For God gave us a spirit not of fear but of power and love and self-control.

2 Timothy 1:7 ESV

Fear is a powerful tool of the enemy. It comes in many varieties and each of us allows at least one type of fear to cripple us, such as the fear of: not being good enough, being judged by others, failure, disease, death, divorce, terrorism, the economy, losing a job, poverty, criticism, losing control, rejection, pain... The list goes on.

Fear keeps us tethered to a pole when we were meant to fly. It stalks us, always lurking in the shadows, waiting for the right time to pounce. More often than not, fear attacks when God is about to use us in a powerful way. Coincidence? Nope! The enemy pulls out all the stops to hinder what God is about to do in, and through, us.

Timothy was young and timid. When Paul wrote this letter to him, he did so to embolden him to continue ministry in Ephesus. And where was Paul when he wrote this letter? Prison—facing his death. He wasn't sitting in his jail cell freaking out or looming over his impending doom. He was praising God, thanking God, trusting God, and writing letters to encourage other people! Who does that? Someone empowered by a Spirit not his own. Someone who does not allow the enemy to use fear to cripple him.

Think about the possibilities, opportunities, and callings in your life that may have been stonewalled by fear. Maybe it was venturing out into a different career, volunteering where there's need, opening up to your spouse, allowing friends into your life, allowing your kids to experience things in which God intends to use to build them up but you're too scared to let go, talking to someone about your faith, joining a small group that will challenge you? Whatever it is, take that bull by its horns and bring it down. You have the power of Paul and Timothy. The same power that was in them is also in you.

Reflection: What fears do you face? What silly, irrational fear do you have? What is a deep, disabling fear that you have? In what ways has this fear crippled you? If fear were not in the picture, how would your life be different?

Prayer: Father, God, thank you for so generously giving me power over my fears. Please release my fears and help me remember that I do, indeed, have power over them. I ask that, in all circumstances, you would give me the same peace and joy Paul experienced in the most difficult times of his life. Amen.

Worship: "Fear Is A Liar" by Zach Williams and "Live Alive" by Rend Collective

21

The Weapon of Power Within

For God gave us a spirit not of fear but of power and love and self-control.

2 TIMOTHY 1:7 ESV

Fear blocks us from the abundant gifts God longs to give us. To experience all God has for us, we must give fear the final smack down. Paul teaches us about three things we have in our arsenal to combat fear: power, love, and self-control. What an arsenal of weaponry in our possession to go against fear! Here, in the second part of the study of 2 Timothy 1:7, we'll learn about power. Then, we'll take on love and self-control in Parts 3 and 4.

Let's not underestimate Satan's power. He can and will knock us off our feet. His power outweighs us humans in our natural state. In Satan's pride and greed, he went to war with God, using earth, particularly Christians, as his battlefield (Revelation 12). His plan on earth is to seek out people, beloved by God, and destroy them (1 Peter 5:8). However, let's not *overestimate* his power over us either. Jesus revoked Satan's power over anyone who claims Christ (Colossians 2:13-15). God equips us with armor for defense and calls us "more than conquerors" (Ephesians 6:10-18, Romans 8:37). Satan knows his limitations, but he doesn't want *us* to know, or use, this power against him. So, Satan speaks lies, the lies of fear we discussed in the prior devotion, hoping we won't remember our weaponry against him.

Let's take an inventory of the powerful weapons we have over evil:

Power to Overcome: We are more than conquerors (Romans 8:37). If God can promote Joseph from prisoner to second-in-command over a powerful nation, and if he can elevate David, a simple shepherd boy, from fugitive to king, oh the possibilities for what he's going to do with you!

Power over Sin: God broke the chains of sin empowering us to overcome the sin that binds us (Romans 8:1-4, 1 Corinthians 10:13, Hebrews 2:18).

Power over Evil: God provides us with weapons against the powers in the dark spiritual world. He lists those weapons as truth, righteousness, peace, faith, salvation, the Word of God, and prayer (Ephesians 6:10-18). Christians are given a power not given to others (Acts 19:11-20).

Power in Prayer: We have the privilege of being heard by the God of all creation and confidence to receive what we ask for when we ask according to his will. God moves in power when we pray. Our prayers can even impact God's actions, at times (James 5:16, John 9:31, 1 John 5:13-15, Genesis 18:27-33).

On our own, we are unsuccessful at overcoming some of life's struggles. We don't beat the patterns of sin and addiction, and we cannot make evil flee. However, as Christians, we have a power that is not our own, the Holy Spirit in all his power, imbedded right into us. When Christ died, we died to ourselves along with him. When Christ arose, so did we. When Christ was seated at the right hand of God, we were also seated with him (Ephesians 2:5-6). We are in rhythm with Christ and have his power.

Remaining in step with this Supreme Being takes time, effort, prayer, denial of self over and over, worship, quiet listening, realigning our perspectives, and our obedience. Satan knows that if he can distract us from that connection, he can debilitate us and bring us harm. Don't let him distract you! Recall our prisoner friend, Paul. He could have let fear hinder him, but instead, he chose to use the God-given power within him. Remember you have that same power!

Reflection: Are you finding old sin hanging on in your life? Are you letting Satan harass you or lie to you? How can you use this God-given power to combat evil? Which power listed above needs put into play more often in your life?

Prayer: Powerful God, I come to you, knowing full well I am powerless over evil on my own. Thank you for allowing me a slice of your premium power to overcome trials, temptations, deception, and anything and everything that holds me back from the good gifts you have for me. Help me to remember when I feel trapped, that you have overcome. Make me an overcomer as well! Amen.

Worship: "Same Power" by Jeremy Camp and "Breakthrough Miracle Power" by Passion (feat. Kristian Stanfill & Tauren Wells)

22

The Weapon of Love

For God gave us a spirit not of fear but of power and love and self-control.

2 TIMOTHY 1:7 ESV

Among the powerful weapons in our arsenal against fear, we have love. We don't typically think of love as a weapon, but it is, in fact, fierce when wielded against the enemy's lies. In its fullest capacity, it can drive out and defeat the author of that fear. We are told in 1 John 4:18, "There is no fear in love. But perfect love drives out fear..."

Some say every action we take is motivated either by love or by fear. Why do you clean the house? Because you love your family or because you're afraid someone will drop in and pass judgement? Why do you buy your wife a Valentine's gift? Because you love her or because you fear the "doghouse"? Why do you do a good job at work? Because you love God and are called to work at it as if working for God and not for man (Colossians 3:23) or because you fear losing your job? Making decisions out of fear is not the "safe" or loving choice but the defensive choice. When we live in this constant state of defense, we become weary and lose the battle against fear, leaving our spirits exhausted and spent. The only countermeasure to fear is to let love be in command. Only then will our peace be restored and leave us rest. Only then, when we have wielded the weapon of love, will fear be defeated.

The Bible likens us to sheep. We do have many similarities. Possibly the most striking is that sheep are easily frightened. We are a fearful people and most of what we worry about never transpires. Anxiety and fear are like perpetual, dark clouds in the middle of the day. They obscure the sun which sheds light and gives us clear vision. Those dark clouds of fear limit our perspective. Fear traps us in a hopeless world devoid of love. But the sunshine of love drives the clouds away, giving us a bright perspective—a true perspective.

Also, perfect love drives out fear because there is security in knowing we are loved with an everlasting love (Jeremiah 31:3). Furthermore, there is security in knowing God makes all things work together for the good (Romans 8:28). Sometimes, I come out of my alone time with God feeling such a deep connection with him, like I can take on the world. *Nothing*, not any worry or fear I'm dealing with, is too much for me when my knowledge of his love has taken root in my heart.

When we find our security in him, we no longer fear death because we will then finally be home. We no longer fear failure because we know we're enough for the only one who matters. We no longer fear catastrophic events because we know who holds it all together and works the seemingly bad into truly good.

Fear comes knocking on our door, sometimes in the middle of nowhere. We're happily busy with a hobby we enjoy when the dark clouds of fear start rolling in. Telling fear to go away is not always effective. Fear asks something of us—our acknowledgement, a solution, something—before it will go away. We need to give it the attention it seeks, however, within containment. There is a healthy worry and an unhealthy worry. A healthy worry takes a possible outcome and gives it a practical, possible solution—a solution that includes divine intervention because God always intervenes. He always takes our brokenness and gives it beautiful purpose. Once we tell our problems how big our God is, then we feel safe to let fear go. Allowing the fear to recycle through our heads with no solutions is unhealthy.

Designate a certain time of day each day when you will allow yourself to contemplate your fears, preferably right before or after your alone time with God. When fear unexpectedly rolls in, tell it the time of day it will get your attention, then pay it no heed until that time. If it continues pestering, write it down. Sometimes acknowledging it in writing gets it out of your head, allowing your mind to relax. When it is fear's assigned time to enter your mind, give it the acknowledgement it demands, brainstorm for solutions, and most important of all, pray over it. Then, don't give it a voice again until that set time the next day. Eventually, as God gives you new perspective through prayer, those fears will fade.

The Bible tells us not to fear three-hundred sixty-five times. Coincidence? God knows our daily struggle. He has the cure. Love. Our security in God's love means fear cannot rock our boats.

Reflection: Have you ever come out of time in God's presence with a new sense of security? How long are you typically able to hold on to that before it fades? What time of day can you designate to acknowledging fear? Decide you're not going to let it out of containment until that time each day. At that time, pray over it and then lock it up again.

Prayer: Loving Father, I confess that I worry too much over undeserving concerns. You commanded me not to fear in so many different ways, by so many different authors, over so many thousands of years, and yet, here I am, allowing fear to grip me on the daily. God, teach me to sit in your presence, to walk in step with you, to grasp your everlasting love, so nothing else in the world can shake me. Amen.

Worship: "Stand In Your Love" by Bethel Music and "I Will Look Up" by Elevation Worship

23

The Weapon of Self-Control

For God gave us a spirit not of fear but of
power and love and self-control.

2 TIMOTHY 1:7 ESV

How is self-control a weapon against fear? "Like a city whose walls are broken through is a person who lacks self-control" (Proverbs 25:28). Without self-control, we are compared to a city ransacked by the enemy. When we lack self-control, we lose big. Self-control protects the gifts God gives us, one of which is the power of the mind.

Our minds are gifts from God, offering us more power than we realize. A study in *Psychology Today* stated, "Neurotransmitters control virtually all of the body's functions, from feeling happy to modulating hormones to dealing with stress. Therefore, our thoughts influence our bodies directly because the body interprets the messages coming from the brain to prepare us for whatever is expected."[3] Our thoughts control both how we feel and how we respond to the world around us. Along with this powerful tool, God gave us free will over what we choose to think about. Although we can't control those thoughts that are like pop-up ads, we can choose to "click on" them and explore them further, or ignore them.

There are several ways we can use the weapon of self-control to overpower the beast of fear:

Having a Heart of Gratitude: Having a mind of gratitude literally rewires the brain to eliminate anxious triggers.

Throwing Out Negative Self-Talk: Anxiety feeds on negativity: feelings of low self-worth (*Nobody likes me. I have no value or place in this world.*), guilt (*I could have done more to prevent this.*), focusing on the one thing that went wrong rather than all that went right (*Even though my presentation got rave reviews, I tripped on my way to the stage.*), making predictions about worst-case scenarios *(My son isn't home yet; he must have been in a car accident.*) Our negative thoughts usually are not accurate and they're hurting us, not helping us. We wouldn't tell our friend she's a failure because she forgot one minor detail or tell our child, since his dad isn't home on time, he might have had a heart attack and died instantly. It's unthinkable! So why do we talk to ourselves that way?

Maintaining Consistent Sleep Patterns: Poor sleep contributes to depression and anxiety. Taking control over the unnecessary things that keep us up late (gaming, TV, hobbies) and being intentional about a responsible bedtime, reduces anxiety.

Changing Diet: Food affects mood! Changing our diet requires self-control and, as we have seen, self-control deals a hard blow to fear. Many foods contribute to anxiety: caffeine, sugar, gluten, dairy, soda (both regular and diet), light dressings, aspartame, and alcohol. Plenty of other foods reduce anxiety: fish, vegetables, blueberries, almonds, Brazil nuts, eggs, turmeric, chamomile, and green tea. Also, drinking plenty of water helps as dehydration affects mood and thoughts.

Exercising: The benefits of exercise are God's gift to us. It is a natural and effective anti-anxiety treatment without the negative side effects of medications! It reduces tension and stress, raises both physical and mental energy, and releases endorphins which make us feel all around better. Again, it is self-control that keeps us in a regular pattern of exercise leading to reduced fear.

Breathing Exercises: Deep breathing stimulates the parasympathetic nervous system, which causes a state of relaxation. Taking controlled breaths lowers anxiety.

Avoiding/Limiting Time With Negative People: There may be people in your life who provoke anxiety in you. They have a negative outlook on life, are pessimistic, and are always verbalizing the worst-case scenarios. This attitude is contagious and destructive. Avoiding or limiting time spent with Negative Nancy may give you another notch up with anxiety.

Limiting Time Spent Watching the News: Studies show, watching the news for just fifteen minutes increases anxiety. I'm not saying to stick your head in the sand and remain oblivious to world events. However, if you're one who struggles with anxiety, consume small amounts of news once a day and routinely follow it up with breathing exercises and prayer.

Becoming Others-Focused: Being sincerely happy for others' success, complimenting others, and showing kindness, grace, and generosity to them are all ways to rewire the brain, ultimately bringing us out of our anxiety.

If God commands us not to fear, why would we spend time participating in fear-inducing activities, avoid exercise, and allow negative self-talk? God gave to us self-discipline as a weapon to defeat the enemy of fear, yet we choose not to pick up our sword and use it. Satan makes the couch, chips, soda, and twenty-four/seven news appear like a great way to relax. It's a lie! It's a trap that causes us to fall into the pit of anxiety. Take up your weapon of self-control and triumph over the enemy of fear.

As Christians, we should excel in self-control. It is a fruit of the Spirit which comes along with our belief in God. While our bodies and minds have a natural bent for doing our own thing, the Spirit of God harnesses and tames us. The closer we come to God, the more uncomfortable we feel when we're outside his will. The more we understand the direction God is moving, the less inclined we are to walk away, towards the traps of anxiety. The difference between control as the world defines it and control by the Spirit of God—one leads to self-gratification and our demise and the other to freedom from fear and safety within the boundaries of God's love.

Do you think self-control is an important part of a marriage relationship? Does it make sense then, that self-control is an important component in our relationship with God? If we need more self-control, we can ask for more from the one who gives it freely and we can learn to sync our steps with him who helps us maintain it.

Reflection: Have you ever been able to change an outcome by worrying? How has worrying hurt you? Out of the nine listed ways to reduce fear/anxiety, how many are already a part of your daily routine? How have these habits helped you or changed you? Which of the above self-disciplines that you are not currently using will you use to combat anxiety?

Prayer: Father, God, I thank you for giving me such a powerful tool along with the free will to use it. I know it is not your will for me to fear or to struggle with anxiety. I pray you teach me to use self-control to conquer my fear and anxiety. When I'm tempted to "relax" with fear-inducing activities, give me the wisdom and ambition to change my habits. Teach me to walk in step with you. Amen.

Worship: "The One" by Aaron Shust and "Still" by Rend Collective

24

Designed for Interdependence

Carry each other's burdens, and in this way you will fulfill the law of Christ.
GALATIANS 6:2

I love the saying, "Not my circus. Not my monkeys." It's freeing to think another person's drama is not our own. However, the heartaches and suffering of other people and their tragic circumstances *are* our circus and those people *are* our monkeys. God's Word instructs us to die to "self" and take on the burdens of others alongside them.

We live in a culture of selfishness. Self-care is highly promoted. While taking care of oneself is a good thing, it becomes problematic when we are caught in self-absorption and fail to care about the burdens of others. Worse yet, we fail to even *notice* the heartache that surrounds us. This is the "me first" mentality. If it's inconvenient or doesn't serve a purpose, if it interferes with my peace or is uncomfortable, if there's nothing in it for me or if it doesn't bring joy, pay it no heed for it's not my circus. However, that's not the way God created us to live.

We were not designed to be completely self-reliant. Movies like *Cast Away* and *Into the Wild*, show us the damaging effects of self-reliance. Scripture teaches us another way. It tells us to "carry each other's burdens." The Greek word for *burden* is *baros*, which conveys a weight that is heavy or crushing. Have you ever felt that way? Have you felt like you've carried a weight so heavy, you could fall under it and be crushed? When someone is under a pressing weight, it is the responsibility of others to stoop into that burden and carry it with them. Yes, we get messy. Yes, it's hard work. Yes, it is inconvenient. Yes, it may require all the strength we have to lift it, but lift it together we must. That is our calling.

The purpose of the book of Galatians was to confront people who were falling into legalism, the strict adherence to self-imposed laws or an attempt to gain salvation through good works. It's as if Paul, the writer, were saying, *If you want to be preoccupied with obeying the law, to the point of making your lives more difficult, instead preoccupy yourselves with taking the burdens off your neighbor.* If you have become preoccupied with "doing good works" for the sake of earning salvation or have become too distracted by selfishness, consider Paul's call to carry another's burden. Paul assures us this will "fulfill the law of Christ." What law? The second greatest commandment, to love our neighbor as ourselves.

Reflection: On a scale with *self-reliance* on one end and *depending on others for help* on the other, toward which side do you lean? What keeps you from helping others? Think of a time you felt a crushing burden until someone came alongside you and helped you. Where would you be if they hadn't? Consider thanking them for it.

Prayer: Thank you, God, for not setting us up for failure due to complete self-reliance. Thank you for placing us in each other's lives that we might come to know the joy of bearing one another's burdens. When I am tempted to believe I don't need others and when I am tempted to believe others brought on their own problems and, therefore, should carry them alone, please forgive me and change me. Teach me to live in community as you have established. Amen.

Worship: "I Refuse" by Josh Wilson and "Love Come To Life" by Big Daddy Weave

25

How to Carry the Burdens of Others

Carry each other's burdens, and in this way you will fulfill the law of Christ.

GALATIANS 6:2

God created people with a craving for purpose. Without purpose, we are more likely to suffer depression. According to *Journal of Medical Psychology*, research shows striving to help others and making a positive difference in others' lives, improves depression.[4] So, in a way, helping others is a form of self-care!

Serving others gets our minds off our own perils for a bit to focus on someone else. Sometimes, when we stoop in to help others bear their crushing burdens, our own burdens come into proper perspective. We may realize our own troubles are not as crushing as we had imagined.

Sometimes perspective does no good because our burden truly is bigger than another's, but it's refreshing to take a break from our own and focus on another's. When I was going through cancer treatments, so much focus was on my problem for such a long time. It was refreshing to go to the house of a friend-of-a-friend, who knew nothing of my problem, and pray with her over her special-needs child and brainstorm with her how to set up her house in a way to meet his needs. Unless we are unconscious, we can help another through encouragement and prayer. We can't minimize the power they hold.

Everyone we meet is carrying a burden. All around us people deal with divorce, eviction, disease, parenting a child who is bullied or has a disability, addictions, poverty, broken friendships, job loss, rebellious children, the loss of a loved one, watching a loved one suffer, being lied about to others, clinical depression, mental illness, or loneliness.

Sometimes, we feel compassion for others and want to help but don't know what to do. Often, in our inability to see how to help, we do nothing. How can we show up for others and lift their burdens? Approaches are endless. Here are a few ideas: landscape for the single mom, pack up the house for someone going through a divorce, give a financial donation to those having trouble paying bills, babysit or mentor a friend's kids, run to the store for a friend who is struggling to keep up or confined to the house (usually they will say they don't need anything, so word it like this, "I'm going to the store. Send me a list of some things you need."), send encouraging texts throughout the day, make a meal, take them a care package, give a long hug, take a pick-me-up treat to their work or home, take them out to talk, or just be present for them. Sometimes simply our presence, even in silence, is enough.

Here are a few dos & don'ts of carrying others' burdens: Don't give unwelcomed advice. It can come across as judgmental. Don't say you understand how they feel when you really don't. No two crises are alike—every burden is unique. You may have experienced a similar situation and have helpful and encouraging words; however, others may feel like you are just trying to "top" their situation. Although sharing may give them hope, don't *monopolize* the conversation with your similar experience. This makes it all about you when it's not. Be sensitive to the situation and to the other person's feelings. Ask God to help you be sensitive to whether advice is desired or obnoxious. Ask the other person, "Do you want to know about my experience with this? Or do you just want me to listen?" Don't say things like, "I'm here if you ever need me," or "Please let me know if there's anything I can do." These are empty offers. It puts the ball in their court while you feel you "covered" it. A person in dire need is not going to call and ask for help. Their need is so great, it is all they can see. It's like expecting someone who has just fallen and hit the pavement to call 911 themselves and tell the paramedics how to treat them. Lastly, follow-up is essential. Mark it on your calendar to check up on them in the near future.

Praying for others is powerful and is commanded in Scripture. Knowing someone cares enough to pray for us can lighten some of the load. However, solely praying for them can become an excuse to stay out of their mess. *If I tell you I'm praying for you, then I don't have to show up for you.* Pray diligently for them, and then show up for them too.

Reflection: Who do you know is carrying a heavy burden? In what way can you lift that burden with them? Put it in your calendar right now.

Prayer: Father, thank you for those in my community who have lifted a burden from me [list them out]. Help me to be sensitive to others' needs, to be able to see through the masks they wear, and into their deep needs. Give me the time, wisdom, and energy to help others and give me insight into how I can lift their burdens. Thank you for giving us one another in community. Amen.

Worship: "Look Like Love" by Britt Nicole and "Instrument" by Matt Maher

26

Beauty in Our Crushed Clay Pot

But we have this treasure in jars of clay to show that this all-surpassing power is from God and not from us. We are hard pressed on every side, but not crushed; perplexed, but not in despair; persecuted, but not abandoned; struck down, but not destroyed.

2 Corinthians 4:7-9

In the ancient near east, clay jars were used to store one's wealth. When saving for something costly, like a field, they would bury the clay pots with their coins inside. These clay pots were commonplace and had little value, but they were made to hold a treasure. This is the comparison Paul uses to describe *us*. Unlike a gold treasure chest adorned with jewels, clay pots are plain and simple. Similarly, we are nothing outstanding. It's the treasure inside giving us worth, and that treasure is God himself.

Hard pressed. That is the way God expects us to live. He never promised our lives would be easy. In fact, we're guaranteed trials (John 16:33). We don't even get to choose which trials. We just ride the waves coming at us. The hope this Scripture brings is that even though we are pressed from every side, we can have confidence we won't be destroyed in the process. Many pots break under pressure, but not us! In fact, he uses our hardships to show others we are different and to show himself through us. God wants to show himself to the world through a different attitude and a different way of reacting to suffering. Others who see us hard-pressed, going through trials yet not breaking, can see we have a superhuman strength in an atmosphere of great pressure. We are still holding on to our joy and peace. We show others good can come out of suffering.

Jesus abandoned his place in Heaven and came to earth as a "clay jar." He was crushed for our transgressions, hard-pressed on the cross, felt the physical pain from beatings and the emotional pain of rejection. He was willing to lose his life and trusted God not only to bring it back but to bring about something significant from his suffering. God came through! Jesus's death and resurrection were so significant that we are still astounded by him 2,000 years later! The power was not in his "clay jar," but in his message.

Just as Jesus died so that we could be given life, when we die to our selfish desires, others are given life. In our sacrifices, others flourish. We are called to superhuman acts such as loving our enemies, forsaking vengeance, and doing good to those who don't deserve it. Sometimes it feels as though we're dying inside due to all the pressure and heartache, but our brokenness is where God speaks with the most impact. The "pressing" causes our message to blare loudly. And he doesn't leave us there in our pain. Joy comes in the morning. Beauty is made from ashes. A joyous blessing rises from our mourning. A heart of praise, not of despair, comes from our faith. All of these are promised to us in Isaiah 61:3. That is the treasure we carry in our clay pot.

Reflection: Can you think of someone who is an ace at demonstrating joy and peace throughout their suffering? What do you think gives them this strength? What ways, in past times of distress, have you seen positive come from pain? What specific troubles are you going through right now? How do you think God can use this to show himself powerful?

Prayer: Father, God, thank you that even though it feels I might be crushed, you always pull me through. Thank you that my suffering is not wasted. Thank you for giving me such a significant purpose of holding this treasure inside me. Please help me trust that you are going to make something good out of my difficulties and pain. I pray my life would be a megaphone to blare your message loudly. Amen.

Worship: "Bruises" by Holly Starr and "Let Them See You" by Colton Dixon

27

Fear of Man

Fear of man will prove to be a snare, but
whoever trusts in the LORD is kept safe.

PROVERBS 29:25

Fear is a trap. Paralyzing us, it prevents us from pushing forward and accomplishing great things. Our boundaries in life are set by our fears. So, trapped in the clutches of fear is a place God does *not* want us to be. All throughout Scripture, God commands us not to fear. Proverbs 29:25 warns against a certain kind of fear—the fear of man.

There are many common ways we have "fear of man": fear of what others think, fear of judgement (perceived or real), fear of rejection, fear of the consequences of going against popular opinion, fear of being manipulated, fear of becoming the subject of gossip, fear of government, fear of sharing our faith. Powerful and crippling, fear controls our behavior and interferes with our relationships and personal growth.

In some violent, less-protected cultures, "fear of man" can mean fearing the physical harm others can do to us—beatings, rape, and murder. In some countries, "fear of man" can mean fearing persecution, even execution, for one's faith. For most Americans today, our "fear of man" comes in the form of fearing rejection, manipulation, gossip, and judgements. We want to be loved and accepted; however, attaining and sustaining the approval of *everyone* is not achievable and the effort to do so is exhausting. We can be the sweetest peach, but there's always going to be someone who hates peaches! And that's okay. It can be hard to get past a peach-hater's hurtful words when they spew out their disgust of peaches.

However, sometimes we've become a rotted peach. We all have flaws and can, like fruit, bruise and taste rotten. At times it would do us well to listen to the reprimands of others rather than fear them, and welcome words meant for our personal growth. God sometimes uses others' words to sharpen us "as iron sharpens iron," or in this case, "sweeten." However, if we've considered the reprimand with an open mind and found it to be untrue, remember some people just don't like peaches. God may be saying *Child, you shut that out. Those discouraging words are not from me. You are loved tremendously just as you are.*

To shut out other people's opinions, we must stay plugged in to God's Word and remind ourselves often of his promises and our value to him. We tend to be so forgetful of his love for us. It's a good idea to write Scriptures of his love and his promises and then to post them in a place we will see them daily. Memorize them. Listen to worship music that may get stuck in our heads and continue reminding us of who we are. Surround ourselves with other faith-filled people who will remind us of what God thinks of us.

We are defined by whose approval we want. Are we focused on other people's opinions? Or are we focused on identifying as a beloved child of God? It's all about *whose* we are.

Reflection: What "fears of man" do you have? How can you remember to shut out the destructive words of others and focus on the life-giving words of God? Which idea for reminding yourself of *whose you are* and your value to him will you implement in your life?

Prayer: Loving Father, thank you for teaching me it's only your truth about me that matters. Sometimes I let others' words cut deep into my soul. Thank you for teaching me in your Word exactly how to overcome my fear of man. I pray you will help me take hurtful words in stride and to remember you only want me to take to heart what you have written in your Word about me. I pray my words would not be the cause of someone else's fear. May I be careful with the way I speak to others and with sharing my opinions. Amen.

Worship: "This Is Me" by Selah and "Human Condition" by Unspoken

28

Fear of Man and Social Media

Fear of man will prove to be a snare, but whoever trusts in the LORD is kept safe.

PROVERBS 29:25

Social media has launched us into a whole new level of "fear of man." Studies indicate there is a strong correlation between social anxiety and social media. Before we decide to delete social media altogether, let's remember it has its perks. It allows us an easy way to stay connected with family and friends who live far away. It's a quick way for news on our lives to spread to multiple people at once. We can find community and support groups for a particular situation. It provides many opportunities for ministry—to spread positivity, to encourage others, to become aware of others' needs, and to organize and provide support for those in need.

A major problem with social media, however, is that it's what many of us turn toward to find acceptance. But we won't find it there. So where should we find it? Proverbs 29:25 tells us to find it by trusting in the Lord.

I go through seasons, as do we all, with the state of my emotional tank. Sometimes I'm feeling good and confident, and my emotional tank is full. At these times, I can easily scroll through my social media feed, feel inspired by the positive posts and scroll right past the negative posts without my mood taking a nose-dive. There are other times, however, when my emotional tank is low and social media only further depletes me. Those are the times I need to take a social media fast. During my fast, at the times I would normally pop on social media, I instead pop into the Word, filling myself only with what God thinks of me until my emotional tank is full enough to scroll past the negativity unphased. It may only be one day. It may be several weeks. I encourage you to do the same when your emotional tank is running on empty.

One of my favorite meditations when I'm on empty is *The Father's Love Letter* by Barry Adams. It has been made free and easily accessible through a printable PDF and, also, through a song set to music. It's a great way to refresh our God-given-image. Our emotional tank can only be sustained by him.

Reflection: How does social media affect your mood? How does it affect your ~~self image~~ God-given-image? One way of conquering "fear of man" is fasting from social media and replacing that time with the Word. In what other ways can you conquer your "fear of man" that stems from social media?

Prayer: Loving Father, I so easily forget how much you love me and how much that should matter to me. When you are for me, who can be against me? Thank you for your pure acceptance of me. I pray I would rely on that alone to keep the wind in my sails. When I'm feeling low, remind me that trusting you is the safest place to remain. May that be enough for me. I pray I would not contribute to the negativity in the world, but instead, spread salt and light. Amen.

Worship: "The Father's Love Letter" by Barry Adams and "Hungry (Falling On My Knees)" by Vineyard Worship, Joy Williams, or MercyMe (Simply called "Hungry" by MercyMe)

29

Our Opinions & Stubbornness

Fools find no pleasure in understanding but delight in airing their own opinions.
PROVERBS 18:2

Think about the way we humans enter the world, without knowledge of how to use even our own hands, but quickly finding a way to boldly scream to others. Even as we develop into children and teens, we can barely see outside ourselves. Conveniently, our opinions are usually self-serving. Some of us are stuck in that early stage of uninformed and selfish opinions, not aware or simply not caring enough, to look at the big picture before drawing our conclusions. It's not until we mature and develop a sense of those around us that we seek to understand others and allow change in our opinions.

Opinions are often formed without graciousness or consideration. It could be, when you're running late to your meeting, the slow driver in front of you is not being inconsiderate but is just coming back on the road after a bad accident. It could be your unfriendly or forgetful waitress is not incompetent but rather in the process of a bad break up. It could be your wife wants to talk through your whole movie, not because she wants to annoy you, but because she really needs your company and connection. How often do we come to a judgment based on what Person A says about Person B, only to get to know Person B and find that Person A's opinion was selfishly skewed?

When we withhold our opinions in favor of grace, we often gain a new understanding of the situation, and it shifts our judgement. Understanding is a floodlight that dispels the darkness of judgement. It's best to give the benefit of the doubt to others freely, graciously, and automatically.

Having strong opinions goes hand-in-hand with stubbornness. Stubbornness does have some beneficial qualities—the ability to persevere when the odds are against us, not allowing the impossible to deter our efforts, and inspiring others to persevere, as well, come to mind. However, stubbornness can be damaging. Without having the whole picture, we can be fueled with unnecessary anger against those who don't agree with us. We are deterred from asking for help when we really need it. We don't admit we're in the wrong or take responsibility for our own wrong-doings.

In our stubbornness, we often think if another person can change our minds, we are indecisive and cowardly. Having the ability to change our minds after discovering new information does not make us spineless and wishy-washy. It makes us wise. It's okay to say, *I don't know enough about this to form an opinion.* It doesn't make us weak-minded, but mature, thoughtful, introspective, and wise. Others will regard our opinions highly when they know we are guided by grace and understanding.

Ephesians 4:29 says, "Do not let any unwholesome talk come out of your mouths, but only what is helpful for building others up according to their needs, that it may benefit those who listen." Let's think about how our opinions will affect the people around us. Our opinions may be true, but will they build someone up? If not, let's be wise and keep them to ourselves.

Reflection: Do others consider you to be an opinionated or stubborn person? Look at the paragraph listing the pros and cons of stubbornness (fourth paragraph). Do you see any of those negative or positive qualities in yourself? Think about the strong opinions you hold. In what situation might you have been uninformed of all the details and wrongly accused someone? In what situations can you offer the benefit of the doubt? How can you build others up with your opinions?

Prayer: Father, forgive me when I have drawn conclusions based on my limited knowledge. Forgive me for placing so much worth on my opinions that it has wedged its way between my relationships and caused division. Help me to keep my mouth shut when my opinion will not build another up. I pray I would maintain the good qualities of stubbornness and dispose of the negative. Amen.

Worship: "Love Anyway" by Tenth Avenue North and "The Strength To Let Go" by Switchfoot

30

Pleasure in Understanding

Fools find no pleasure in understanding but delight in airing their own opinions.

Proverbs 18:2

We can gather from Proverbs 18:2 that, unless we are fools, we will find pleasure in understanding. When we seek to understand, our desire to gain knowledge and insight is stronger than our desire to air our own opinions. How many of us can honestly say we would rather understand other people than share our own thoughts, opinions, and where we stand on things? It's a lofty goal but this verse suggests we'll find pleasure on our journey there.

Seeking to understand means we strive to gain insight into others' lives, motivations, and viewpoints. Consequently, we give grace when we would otherwise judge. Sometimes we forget how painful it felt to be misunderstood or judged. At one point, we were judged—we wanted to give insight into our lives and dismiss the false accusations. We would do well to remember how that felt—to put ourselves in another's shoes—for then we can offer to others what we had longed for—understanding and grace.

Seeking to understand means we listen more than we talk—listen to learn and gain insight rather than "listen" to form a response. Listen by asking questions of others, not for the purpose of "poking holes" in their argument, but for gaining a new perspective. Even if we ultimately don't agree with the other perspective, there is joy and peace when we attempt to "see" others. There is joy when we give people a piece of our heart rather than a piece of our mind.

Seeking to understand means we are open to looking at ourselves as others might perceive us. It's easy to give others the wrong impression. My face doesn't usually match my heart and thoughts. When I came to understand my face gives off an angry expression when I'm deep in thought (even deep in thought about something positive), I could work on lightening my expression and becoming more intentional about smiling.

If it's so easy for others to get the wrong idea about us, consider how easy it is for us to get the wrong impression of others. Again, insight and understanding lead to grace.

Maybe others are wrong. But maybe *we're* wrong. When we're clearly in the wrong, brushing it under the rug doesn't make us look less wrong. It makes us look prideful. There is no pleasure in being corrected and seeing our wrong. Not at first. But there is even less pleasure when others avoid us because we can't look at our wrongdoings and self-improve. What the world desperately needs is for each of us to have a better attitude about correction. When confronted with the idea that our ways, thoughts, or opinions are wrong, instead of instantly putting up our defenses and spewing out excuses, let's make it a habit to initially not respond at all. Take a few days, after a confrontation, to question it and pray about it. Let's have the courage to ask someone else, a close friend who will tell us the truth in love, before we chuck the idea. With this habit of openness and self-evaluation, may we find others desire, instead of dread, our presence. There is pleasure in that.

Another way to gain understanding, is to surround ourselves with people who are wise. Ask them questions and observe their interactions with others. I was touring the Florida Everglades when we came across a deer standing in a mucky pond up to the top of his legs. He had green plants and pond moss across his back, dripping down his sides. The tour guide told us he had been abandoned as a baby and was raised by the water buffalo. He became a part of their herd and he thought he was a water buffalo! In the same way, we become like those with whom we surround ourselves. If we hang with those who air their opinions without interest in gaining insight into others' viewpoints, we are limiting ourselves to mucky ponds. If we are intentional about spending time with those who seek to learn from others, to love and accept others, and to gain insight into their lives, we will hop and run freely as deer.

Listen. Learn. Gain insight. Self-evaluate. Remain open to correction. Walk in another's shoes. Open your heart to understand another. These are the things that will bring pleasure.

Reflection: Would you say you attempt to truly understand others? Would you say you are open to self-evaluation and correction? Can you think of a recent time you gave someone a piece of your mind? How could you, instead, have given them a piece of your heart? Who in your life do you consider wiser than yourself? How can you be intentional about spending more time with him or her?

Prayer: Dear God, I know you did not promise me a life without difficulty. Instead, you promised to freely give wisdom to any who ask for it. God, I am asking for that wisdom. Please remind me not to jump to conclusions, but to gain understanding. Being criticized makes me feel uncomfortable. However, I pray you will give me the ability to receive criticism constructively. I pray I would not allow criticism to defeat me, but to change me. Help me to find pleasure in understanding. Amen.

Worship: "Revolutionary" by Josh Wilson and "Let Love" by Jesus Culture

31

Active Pursuit of Peace

Let us therefore make every effort to do what leads to peace and to mutual edification.

Romans 14:19

At a time when my children needed daycare for a couple days a week, I was searching for and interviewing daycare providers. I had visited a few in-home daycares that didn't make me feel confident about leaving my children. After going to a house smelling of smoke and another that had terrible "disciplinary" measures, I went home and cried. My husband asked what was wrong. When I told him my frustration, his reply, "Aww, Honey, it will work itself out." (Side note: He has since learned this was the wrong thing to say.) I cried, "No, it won't! You *think* things work themselves out but it's really *me* working them out *for* you." Not too long after, I did find the perfect in-home daycare for our family. In fact, my now-teenage daughter is, to this day, best friends with this former babysitter's daughter and has found in them a second family, even going with them on their family vacations.

Maybe some things, like the kink in your neck, eventually work themselves out. Finding a trustworthy daycare, however, does not. Another thing that does not work itself out is peace within a strained relationship. Simply hoping to stumble upon peace won't have the greatest possible outcome. "Make every effort to do what leads to peace," Paul says. We are to be *actively pursuing* peace. Some translations say to "follow after peace." We are to be peace chasers, to run hard after peace, to fight for peace.

The opposite of fight is flight, or avoidance. Are we running after peace? Or are we passively standing still, hoping peace drops into our laps? When we're at odds with someone, it's excellent to forgive, but we can't just quietly forgive in our hearts and hope the relationship will heal on its own. We are to pursue peace and restore the relationships with the ones we've forgiven. We are to do what it takes, as far as is in our power, to bring that relationship to the point of no tension. Build the bridge and bury the hatchet along with the hostility.

Some think making peace means we must come to an agreement; we must win others to our point of view or there will be no peace. However, if we believe this, we believe a lie. We can disagree and still have peace. When we're staying home from family functions to avoid a family member with differing political or religious views, we have missed the mark. We have lit dynamite under the bridge to peace. If disagreeing adults can have enough respect for one another to listen to the other, listen for the purpose of learning and loving, civil discussions can be eye-opening and educational. However, if emotions run too deep and opinions are too fiercely expressed, it's a good idea to deem that topic off-limits for the sake of peace. Isn't it better to find a common ground to build your relationship than to avoid the relationship altogether?

Reflection: What troubled relationships come to mind today? Have you been hoping it would naturally start moving in a positive direction but haven't taken steps in the pursuit of peace? (If you're ready to take some steps, the next devotion is full of ideas for actively pursuing peace.)

Prayer: God of Peace, thank you for the peace you give, the peace that transcends understanding. Although it feels good when others agree with me, I realize making multiple versions of myself is not your plan. I choose peace in all circumstances because you are the God of Peace and you desire this for my life, my family, and my relationships. Teach me how to actively pursue peace. Bring healing to my broken relationships. Amen.

Worship: "Kingdoms" by 7eventh Time Down, "Pour Me Out" by Brandon Lake, and "Attitude" by Fireflight

32

How to Pursue Peace

Let us therefore make every effort to do what leads to peace and to mutual edification.

Romans 14:19

As we learned in the previous devotion, we are to *actively pursue* peace in all relationships. This is a big calling. Where do we begin? How do we pursue peace with the myriad of people we may not like, may not agree with, and may not even find respectable?

Part of the pathway to peace is prevention. Doves, the symbols of peace, are like any other bird in that any slight commotion makes them fly away. In similar fashion, we must be careful how we speak and act or we'll cause peace to fly out of sight. If the words on the tip of our tongue could wedge us deeper into discord, we need to make an about face. This means we're not going to point out to the one taking offense to what we said that they recently said the same thing to us. We're not going close the door on peace by saying things like, "I'm done with you." We're not going to attack another's character or speak in a way that belittles another, like, "If you side with this view, you're an idiot." We won't immediately shoot down others' ideas, even when they're undoubtedly wrong. If we listen with love and respect and make others believe they are heard, they won't feel the need to escalate.

Many of us wish for peace but are not pursuing the things that make peace. We are holding on to peace slayers such as pride and the need to be right. We have not yet learned that peace is far more deeply satisfying than "being right." Obtaining peace requires humility, self-denial, respect, and loving others more than ourselves. Let's set aside our need to "be right" for the sake of harmony. Sometimes admitting we make mistakes or may have been wrong feels like dying because, well, we're killing our pride. But this death leads to life!

Actively pursuing peace means we aren't waiting around for an apology to make amends. Instead, we apologize first, even if we did nothing wrong. Matthew 5:23-24 directs us to initiate reconciliation, even if it is the other person who has the problem with us. Apologizing moves a conversation in the direction of peace, softens hearts, and disarms those whom, moments ago, stood ready to fire. It may even prompt them to examine their own part in the problem. However, sometimes we don't get their apology, and we have to be okay with that. We need to take whatever sliver of peace the other is willing to offer.

When strong emotions are involved, our perception becomes clouded. We see things that were never there. We hear things that were never said. We must accept there is a very strong possibility both ourselves and those who have wronged us have been misunderstood. We need to leave room for being wrong in our perceptions and give grace to those who've misperceived us.

If our offenders are unaware they have offended us, and aren't continuing to hurt us, it may be best to forgive in our hearts, let go of our grudges in a low-key way, and move forward without bringing it to our offender's attention. Sometimes, to keep the peace, it is best to let sleeping dogs lie. However, if bitterness has settled in, what may appear as a sleeping dog, might be a cat ready to pounce. If that's the case, pursuing peace through a conversation is best.

At times when confrontation is needed to make peace, it's a good idea to have other non-involved people listen to what we plan to say or read what we have written. Ask how the words and tone might come across. Sometimes our thoughts aren't accurately portrayed in the way we say things and can easily be taken the wrong way. If there's even a shred of animosity, it can be communicated unintentionally. Lastly, it's a good idea to ask ourselves three questions before confronting. *Is it kind? Is it true? Is it necessary?*

Sometimes, it's easier not to reconcile with others—just brush it under the rug and move on without the person who rubbed us the wrong way. However, that is our human nature, not God's plan for our lives. When we're in the state of mind we don't even desire reconciliation, we need a heart change. To get to the place we *desire* God's plan for reconciliation, we need to pray for others. Not pray they would change, not pray they would apologize, not pray they would pay for what they did. Pray FOR them. Pray good things will come to them. Pray God's blessings over them. Pray to see them as God sees them. Our own hearts are transformed in a powerful, miraculous way when we pray for those who challenge and stretch us, and we earnestly seek the best for them.

The last part of Romans 14:19 says we are to do what leads to edification.

The Greek for *edification* is *oikodomēs*, which means to build up. Are we building others up or tearing them down? Are we facilitating healing or are we further wounding? Are we instilling confidence or incapacitating? If we're focused on the positive traits in others and giving them encouragement, we're inviting peace to come and stay a while in our lives.

Choose peace. Chase it down. Hold it tightly.

Reflection: What relationships in your life are currently strained? How can you actively pursue peace in those tense relationships? What could you lay aside for the sake of peace? For what good things could you be praying over others who've wronged you?

Prayer: God of Peace, forgive me for the times I have allowed my pride and arrogance to cause tension in my relationships. I lay aside my pride and my need to be right. I pray good things for [name your offender and some good things you hope for them]. Help me to take the right steps toward making amends with them. Soften their heart, and mine as well, so we may establish peace as you wish. Amen.

Worship: "Holy Ground" by JJ Heller and "I Lay Me Down" by Michael W. Smith

33

Loving With Unselfish Motives

If I speak in the tongues of men or of angels, but do not have love, I am only a resounding gong or a clanging cymbal. If I have the gift of prophecy and can fathom all mysteries and all knowledge, and if I have a faith that can move mountains, but do not have love, I am nothing. If I give all I possess to the poor and give over my body to hardship that I may boast, but do not have love, I gain nothing.

1 Corinthians 13:1-3

A rampage of persecution was sweeping through the church at the time of Paul's writing to the Corinthian people, and to this day still rages on in some parts of the world. There were some early Christians who thought their suffering, especially death by martyrdom, was the most important part of being a Christian. But Paul taught them about the importance and priority of love—that without it, nothing is gained. Not only do we gain nothing, we *are* nothing, without love. Love is the absolute most important thing—so important, any sacrifice we make is of no value without it.

There are four words to describe *love* in the Greek language. In this verse, the word *agape* is used. It is a self-sacrificing love given without demands, expectations of repayment, or ulterior motives. It is not given out of pride, for a pat on the back, or for personal gain, and no condition must be met by the receiver. Agape love has little to do with the feeling of love and much to do with self-denial for the sake of another, with another's best interest in mind. It's the acts of service given not only to the easy-to-love but to the obnoxious, intolerable, unlovable *and* that one difficult family member. The second greatest commandment (after the first which is to love God with everything in us) is to love others, *all* of them.

Agape love is awakened when we realize God's agape love for us. We only understand agape love because he agape-loved us first (1 John 4:19). We will never be able to truly agape-love someone until we have first grasped how wide, long, high, and deep is his love and sacrifice for us. When we experience God's love and comprehend our worth, we have so much more agape love to give, not from our broken, empty heart which has been hurt by the world but from a heart completely repaired and filled to its rim by him.

When we think of martyrs, we are so moved by their faith and unswerving commitment to God, we put them on a pedestal—and rightly so! They made the ultimate sacrifice, absolutely everything, including their own earthly lives. But Paul taught us that *anything* done in love, through self-sacrifice without thought of personal gain, no matter how small, is more important than *anything* done for accolades or our own personal gain no matter how grand.

When I think of agape love, I think of those who had nothing to gain from what they forfeited. I think of my friends, Owen and Charlotte, who downsized their house and vacation budget so they would be free to give to any need brought to their awareness. I think of those in my small group, who gave up a Saturday to clean and paint a children's group home. I think of my friend, Lia, who gently steers conversations away from gossip to protect those being gossiped about, even those who have hurt her. I think of Roger, who fights his depression and gets out of bed every day with a forced smile because his family needs him. I think of Faith who makes it a habit to pay for the orders of the people in the car behind her in the drive-through line even though her budget is small.

According to Paul, love surpasses all the gifts we have, all the genuine good we do (gifts, prophecy, knowledge, and faith) and all the insincere good we do (giving with impure motives and suffering for the purpose of receiving admiration). This is pure love. This is our calling.

Reflection: Can you think of a time you made a sacrifice but its purpose was to gain something—admiration, an upward climb for the career, a false kindness with hopes of getting something in return? What gifts or talents have you been given that could be used to love God and others? How could you use that gift with no expectations of personal gain?

Prayer: God, thank you for offering me your unconditional, sacrificial love. May I, in turn, pass that on to others. Show me the gifts and sacrifices you would have me offer. I pray my gifts would not be wasted and used for any purpose suiting my own personal desires. Help me to remember I have nothing, and *am* nothing, without love. May I seize the opportunities you put in front of me to love genuinely. Amen.

Worship: "The Way You Love Me" by Jeremy Camp and "For The One" by Brian and Jenn Johnson with Bethel Music

34

Wasted Actions

If I speak in the tongues of men or of angels, but do not have love, I am only a resounding gong or a clanging cymbal. If I have the gift of prophecy and can fathom all mysteries and all knowledge, and if I have a faith that can move mountains, but do not have love, I am nothing. If I give all I possess to the poor and give over my body to hardship that I may boast, but do not have love, I gain nothing.

1 Corinthians 13:1-3

Maybe you can relate to some of these circumstances:

- A gift given by someone who has dragged your name through the mud. "No thanks, Becky, I don't want a birthday card. I want my reputation back!"
- An invite to a multi-level marketing "party" from a friend who was nonexistent at a time your life hit rock bottom. "Thanks for the invite to buy something, Linda, but where were you when I lost my job and broke my arm immediately following my mother's death?"
- A sexual "gift" from a spouse who never shows you affection outside the bedroom. "Yeah, I'm having trouble getting into it, Bob. My love tank has been starving for months."
- A "preaching" post on social media from someone with a "holier-than-thou" character. "So pleased, Jan, that your ducks are in a neat and orderly row while mine are in a tizzy like a tsunami hit their pond."

How we receive "loving" actions differs depending on the heart of the giver, whether it was given from a heart full of love or from a selfish heart with ulterior motives. When someone tosses us aside or steps on us for their own gain, their loving actions that follow, no matter how grand, don't feel like love at all. Instead, it makes us wonder what's in it for their gain. We then think twice about accepting their "love."

Who makes the most impact in your life?

- A televangelist or the pastor who meets with you weekly and mentors you?
- A boss who simply works for a paycheck or a boss who notices you are not "yourself" and takes the time to find out things are not right at home?
- A dad who is apathetic or one who takes interest in your life?
- A coach who simply cares about physical strength and winning or a coach who invests in the personal growth of your kids?

A dad who is mentally absent while physically present is louder than the silence for it is a resounding gong. A preacher who is out of touch with his people is a clanging cymbal. A mountain mover, one who accomplishes great things, is nothing if he does not love. Potential relationships lost—nothing gained.

The acts of love that are easy to accept center around quality time, focused attention, doing more than is expected, and being intentional. So, if we want others to accept our love, we need to see and love them as God sees and loves them. It is only gifts that come from the unselfish heart with pure motives that leave an impact on our own hearts. Love alone propels the efficacy of our gifts and service.

When being "right" upstages love and compassion, your "rightness" doesn't matter to those around you. You might have everything figured out, but until you love, no one wants your knowledge. You might try to buy your child's love, but it's not for sale. You might think your husband should know he's loved because you clean up after him, cook for him, and wash his laundry, but if most of your words to him are nagging, belittling and void of love, he'll simply feel small, not loved. You might assume your wife knows you love her because you married her, chose to "stick it out" with her, and occasionally help her with housework, but unless you regularly show affection from an overflowing heart instead of a vacant heart, the love is not understood.

Let's make sure our sacrificial actions aren't wasted and agape love prevails.

Reflection: Think of a gift that was hard for you to accept due to the giver's state of heart. What happens when people have power and prestige, give all they have to the poor, move a mountain or two, but have no genuine relationships? How does love affect your witness and relationships? How can you exercise this effectual love from a full, genuine heart?

Prayer: God, sometimes my actions of "love" are self-serving. Fill me with your *agape* love, so my cup overflows with *agape* love for others. May all I do be driven by love. Teach me to impact the world by loving others the way you love. Help me to show others love in the form of genuine compassion instead of vain, empty actions. Amen.

Worship: "Without Love" by Micah Tyler and "The Proof of Your Love" by for KING & COUNTRY

35

Waiting for Love

Love is patient, love is kind. It does not envy, it does not boast, it is not proud.

1 Corinthians 13:4

We're all in love with the idea of love, but the sacrifices we must make to maintain love in our personal lives prove to be challenging. Things like holding our tongue, surrendering our will, parting with something we enjoy, and letting go of offenses, are a few. Sometimes these sacrifices are required to keep something that matters more: relationships.

In a prior devotion, we learned the Greek word for *love* used in 1 Corinthians 13 is *agape*. To recap, agape love is self-sacrificing love. It gives without demands or self-serving expectations. It's given without pride or desire for recognition. It has little to do with the fuzzy feeling of love and much to do with self-denial for the sake of another. Agape love is uncorrupted by selfish motives.

How can we love with such purity? Agape love is awakened when we realize God's love for us. When we remember we sometimes break God's heart but never his love for us or our worth to him. It's from this full-hearted place we can express genuine love for others. Who are we to accept God's love and refuse agape love to others?

Paul further details how agape love is expressed. He doesn't simply give us this lofty goal of agape love and say, "Off you go! Good luck!" His teaching moves farther, right into the daily grind of our everyday lives.

He tells us love is patient. This is not the kind of patience we use when we're in a hurry and stuck in traffic. The Greek word for *patience* used here is a long-tempered type of patience. It is slow to anger, endures offenses without retaliation, gives grace to others when they make mistakes and respects people who have different views. This type of patience attempts to understand others through compassion rather than keeps them at a distance because we can't relate. It desires for others to reach their potential. It patiently waits for maturity without criticism.

Throughout history, God, himself, displays this long-suffering type of patience. The book of Hosea portrays God's patience perfectly. To summarize the story, Hosea was told by God to marry a prostitute, Gomer. Hosea did so, redeeming her from her painful existence, and bringing her into his unmerited love. They were happy and had a son together. But it was not long before Gomer became ungrateful and restless. She broke Hosea's heart as she left him time and time again, chasing other lovers and even bearing children in his house that were not his. God told Hosea to continue taking her back. Then the final blow. Gomer left him again, only this time, she fell into the hands of slave traders. This dreadful day, Gomer was up for sale as a slave. Hosea, under God's instruction, did the unthinkable. Despite his own pain and the shame brought on him by her disloyalty, he bought her from the slave block to make her his wife once again.

This beautiful allegory demonstrates God's loving patience for his people. Hosea represents God, while Gomer represents God's people. Despite our constant rejection of him, God continues to pursue us and buy us back with his ultimate sacrifice for us.

This is the kind of patience God has called us to, not simple tolerance. When God asks us to forgive, to offer grace, and to wait patiently for others to grow, he's not asking us to do something he, himself, hasn't done for us time and time again.

Reflection: Is there a person in your life who requires this long-suffering type of patience from you? How would your relationships look different if you were expressing love with this long-suffering type of patience?

Prayer: God, your patience with me is astounding! I know I've let you down and broken your heart, yet you keep taking me back time after time. Please give me strength to offer second chances (and third and fourth…) and to remain open-hearted to those who have hurt me. I can't do it on my own. I need your help. May I offer grace always and give others the benefit of the doubt. Amen.

Worship: "Coming Home" by Housefires and "Walk In Love" by Elevation Worship

36

Practical Bending

Love is patient, love is kind. It does not envy, it does not boast, it is not proud.

1 Corinthians 13:4

What costs nothing but means everything? Kindness. Paul teaches *agape* love is kind. The Greek word for *kind* Paul used here comes from a word meaning both useful and gentle. So, in essence, kindness searches for opportunities to be useful to others in gentle and practical ways. It bends to become what others need it to be.

There are many, different ways to show kindness. It could be an encouraging comment, whether through a verbal compliment, a handwritten letter, or affirmational text. It could be a listening ear, a shoulder to cry on, a conversation with a stranger who is obviously longing for someone to talk to, a thoughtful gift, a positive comment to brighten someone's day, an allowance for the hurried shopper to cut in line, an invitation to someone not currently in our friend-circle, or a meal for someone under stress.

Opportunities to show kindness are infinite. We will see the needs all around us if we just open our eyes and pay attention to others, whether strangers, friends, or family, we will see the needs in every place we go. Sometimes we see a need but feel at a loss for how to meet the need. We can pray for wisdom in meeting that need, ask others who have been in similar situations what they would have wanted during that time, or research ideas in meeting that need. Sometimes we are surprised, but the smallest gestures can make a world of difference!

Sometimes it takes seeing beyond the surface. My friend, Hannah, while in the bank drive-through, noticed the teller was not up to par and asked, "How's your day?" The teller indicated she was tired and mentioned she was a single mom, wishing she had some support. Hannah came back later that day with a card and money to join a support group for moms. It was love displayed in kindness.

I have been on the receiving end of kindness countless times. Sometimes it was the thing that kept me going when I wanted to throw in the towel. When I was buried in the throes of a difficult parenting situation, a card from a friend came in the mail with words of encouragement that were like balm to my weary soul. When I was diagnosed with cancer, some friends put together a fund-raiser to help me with the unexpected costs. When going through family difficulties, a friend bombarded me with encouraging and funny texts. Kindness comes in all forms, whatever form it needs to bend into, and is a valuable medicine for a hurting world.

Reflection: Recall a time someone extended kindness to you in just the right moment of need. In what practical ways could you show kindness and help others, in the workplace? In your extended family? With your kids? With your spouse? With friends? With a stranger?

Prayer: Kind Father, sometimes I'm oblivious to the needs around me. Open my eyes to the opportunities surrounding me every day. Help me to not be so self-absorbed I miss chances to demonstrate your love to others. When I see someone in need, please show me ways to relieve their burdens, give them hope, and keep them moving forward by blowing a little wind in their sails. Amen.

Worship: "While We Sing" by Leeland and "Less Like Me" by Zach Williams

37

Envy Savage & Boasting Beast

Love is patient, love is kind. It does not envy, it does not boast, it is not proud.

1 Corinthians 13:4

Envy and boasting—these two monsters are related. Envy means *You have it, but I want it.* Boasting says *I have it; don't you wish you did?* Both are ugly and need shown the door in our hearts.

The Greek word for *envy* means to eagerly desire and is rooted in greed and selfishness. Envy wants what others have, either tangible things like wealth, beauty, or a large house or intangible things like success, attention, admiration, a romantic relationship, an intact family, or the friendships others have. It is not wrong to desire such things. It's the disdain we feel toward others who have these things that is wrong. If seeing others with something we lack causes us to feel slighted and upset, we have a problem with envy.

Love is not competitive or seeking "fairness." Love feels genuinely happy for others' successes, possessions, and achievements, even if they are not ours to have. Realizing we don't need these things in order to achieve fulfillment and having gratitude for the things we do have, though it be significantly less, is the way to overcome the beast of envy.

Paul had learned to be content with what he had. For him, whatever he had was enough. In his words to the Philippians, he expressed his contentment in whatever the circumstance, whether in plenty or in want, whether well-fed or hungry. He said the "secret of being content" was learned. I don't think it's a coincidence he ends those thoughts with the famous phrase, "I can do all things through him who gives me strength." Contentment empowers us to do all the things God has called us to (Philippians 4:11-13).

Love does not boast, it is not proud. The Greek word for *boast* describes someone who is full of himself and promotes himself, exaggerating to make himself look more important than others. The Greek word for *proud* means puffed up. While envy wants what others have, pride tries to make others jealous of what *we* have. Boastful, prideful people are annoying, for sure.

Boasters come in many varieties. There's the "low self-esteem" variety: those who have been broken in unhealthy places and need to prove their worth in unhealthy ways. They are afraid of the lies they've bought into about themselves. Though they might believe telling others impressive things about themselves will boost others' perception of them, in time, it has the opposite effect. Then there's the "personal gain" variety: those who attempt to gain higher position or authority through elevating themselves. Sometimes their boasting can appear innocent and subtle but it's boasting all the same. The "center stage" variety: these boasters are always throwing in a story to "top" others' experiences with a better story of their own. They manipulate the conversation to put themselves on center stage. Most of us boast at times and struggle with pride. I think we all can relate to at least one of these types of boasters.

The truth is, we cannot love and boast at the same time. Boasting is centered on *self*, while love has concern for *others*.

The monsters of envy and boasting can be killed using the right weapon. The weapon? Contentment. Finding contentment both in what we have and in who we are. Having gratitude, enjoying the simple things, and expanding our focus to the good we have, are simple ways to bring us contentment and kill these monsters.

Reflection: Is there anything that makes you feel slighted when you see others have it? With which type of boaster can you most relate—low self-esteem, personal gain, or center stage? How can you turn from these types of selfishness and pride? What needs to change for you to have contentment with what you have? List tangible things you are grateful for. List intangible things you are grateful for. Consider how you might expand your focus on these things.

Prayer: Loving Father, sometimes I get this twinge in my heart when I see something others have that I desperately desire. I pray you would transform my heart, so I am genuinely happy for others instead of resentful. I don't want to have selfishness or any kind of pride. It was born along with me, but I need help fighting it every day. Strip away my pride and my need to impress others. Help me to recognize when I'm acting selfishly or trying to boost my approval rating with others. Remind me you love humility and help me to be content in all circumstances. I am thankful for [list out what you are grateful for]. I pray you would establish contentment in me. Amen.

Worship: "I Boast No More" by Caedmon's Call and "My Worth Is Not In What I Own" by Shane & Shane

38

Love Is Not Dishonoring, Self-Seeking, Angry, Bitter

It does not dishonor others, it is not self-seeking, it is not easily angered, it keeps no record of wrongs.
1 Corinthians 13:5

Love does not dishonor others. In Greek, the word for *dishonor* used in this verse means to be unseemly, rude, or not of good form or taste. It is discourteous, insensitive, cares little for the feelings of others, and flippantly disgraces another. We all know this person, and sometimes we *are* this person. Love is polite, courteous, and tactful. It is aware of the customs and traditions of others, showing high regard for people, not because we agree with their customs, but because we love and honor the person.

Love is not self-seeking. The Greek word used in this verse for *self-seeking* describes someone who insists, and even manipulates, to get his own way. To love without seeking our own way means something inside us must die, our will. We must be okay when things go someone else's way. When we are not self-seeking, we take genuine interest in others' points of view, cheer others on, give others credit where it's due, help others achieve their goals, sincerely desire others' success, are quick to listen, and are slow to speak.

Love is not easily angered. The Greek word for this phrase means to stimulate, to rouse to anger, or to be easily provoked. When we're easily angered, we're always ready to erupt. Others feel they must walk on eggshells around us because we're so easily offended. We go off like a bomb, leaving a ruined mess in our wake. We all have buttons that trigger us, but some of us are a big, walking collection of buttons, even taking pride in the buttons, warning others not to bump the buttons. As love is not easily provoked, it has few buttons, and those buttons don't lead to explosions. As my peace-loving son says, "Be triggerless."

We all become angry at times, sometimes justifiably and sometimes not, however, habitual anger is often a sign of something deeper and is destructive to the soul. It can be a manifestation of depression or unresolved pain. Our anger may be, though unknown to us, misplaced. If you are a walking "collection of buttons," it might be time for some outside help from a counselor. There's no shame in getting counseling. We all need it at times. In fact, I have been to counseling for the same. When life gave me repeated lashings, I felt out-of-control and I began snapping at my husband for small things. Talking it out with a counselor helped. No shame in it!

Love keeps no record of wrongs. The Greek word for *keeps record* is an accounting term used to credit one's account. Like accountants, we tally the debits of others' wrong-doings, make a report in our hearts, and sometimes file a "statement" with the one who offended us. This is damaging to our health and prevents healing. Love doesn't bring up offenses after they've been settled, reminding others of the ways they've wronged us. Love doesn't "memory bomb" offenders to reinforce a point. Once settled, it's off the table. Reminding others of their mistakes is an ineffective, unproductive, and damaging way to resolve conflict and maintain relationships. God chooses not to hold our sins against us (Psalm 103:10-12), and he requires us to do the same for others. Choose forgiveness. If you are the kind to journal and you've written down wrongs done to you, burn the journals. They are preventing your healing. Letting go of the journals is an outward sign of an inner letting go.

Reflection: Have you said something to someone in a flippant or insensitive way? Consider apologizing for this. Are you one who is easily offended or "triggered"? If so, can you identify those areas where you may be overly sensitive? Has anger been a part of your daily life? If so, have you considered speaking to someone who can help you get behind your anger? Against whom have you been holding a grudge? In going through these qualities of agape love, which one resonates with you as an area you most need to improve? In what aspects of agape love have you grown the most in the past year?

Prayer: God, thank you for teaching by example, what true love looks like. Help me to be sensitive and tactful with others as I honor them above myself. Remind me of the needs of others when I'm only thinking of myself. Help me to be "triggerless" and to let things go. Teach me to not be rude, self-seeking, easily angered, or a record keeper of wrongs. Only in your power can I do all this. Amen.

Worship: "Be Kind" by The Dailys, Jillian Edwards & Ellie Holcomb and "Open Space" by Housefires

39

Loving What God Loves, Hating What God Hates

Love does not delight in evil but rejoices with the truth.

1 Corinthians 13:6

If you had siblings growing up, you remember tattling on them for hurting you and then basking in the satisfaction of their punishment. It was—and sometimes still is if we're completely honest—gratifying to see those who have hurt us get what's coming to them. We smile a little on the inside when those who've wronged us fail. We've all been tempted to secretly delight in the suffering of those who've wronged us, but that's not love. That's "delighting in evil" and let's call it what it is—sin.

Love does not delight in evil. This means we don't take pleasure in another's pain, no matter how much they deserve it. It doesn't gossip, seek vengeance, or hope for a downfall. We don't have the "right" as Christ followers to that little surge of delight because love is our highest calling.

We need to take a minute here to distinguish between delighting in evil and seeking justice. What is the difference? Is seeking out justice when a woman is raped, a child is murdered, or a hate crime is committed delighting in evil? The answer to this important question is a resounding "no." There is a difference between "delighting in evil" and justice. Delighting in another's suffering is emotional and personal, while justice is rational, impartial, and resolved through the legal system. Love and truth go hand-in-hand, as do truth and justice. Evil prevails when truth is silent. Therefore, it is right to seek justice through the legal system, while forgiving in our hearts and refusing to delight in others' suffering. We are called to mourn evil while forgiving evil-doers.

Love rejoices with the truth. This means celebrating virtuous living, personally walking in the truth, and delighting in the righteousness of others. When an uncle sobers up, a friend quits his job because his coworker was a temptation, a child chooses getting a "D" on a test over cheating to get an "A," this kind of love dissuades against evil and encourages the pursuit of truth. In essence, to not delight in evil but rejoice with the truth, is to hate what God hates and to love what God loves.

Reflection: Think of a time when someone got what was coming to them and your heart was silently pleased. Think of a time you were delighted to witness a loved-one choose truth. Did they know how happy you were for them? In what areas do you feel you love what God loves and hate what God hates? In what areas is it sometimes the other way around?

Prayer: God, forgive me when I'm glad to see others suffer. You don't take pleasure in the suffering of others, even when it was earned. Help me to reflect your heart for others, a heart that desires truth and righteousness, but feels sorrow for suffering. I pray the way I treat others brings out the best in them and causes them to strive for truth and righteousness. Amen.

Worship: "Break My Heart" by Downhere and "Clean Heart" by Matt Maher

40

A Shelter for Others

It always protects, always trusts, always hopes, always perseveres.

1 CORINTHIANS 13:7

Love always protects. The word *protect* in Greek is *stego,* which means to protect by covering, in the way a roof covers a house for protection from bad weather. Like a roof, our love is a shelter over others from the hailstorms beating them up. *Stego* protects others not only physically by providing for their tangible needs, but emotionally and spiritually as well. It supports their need to belong, upholds their character and reputation, and brings them closer to Jesus. Love that always protects looks out for the one who may not feel valued or included. It doesn't go around updating people of the problems of others or sharing things spoken in confidence (Proverbs 17:9). It does not deflate others with painful sarcasm and put-downs or make jokes at another's expense. Love defends the character of others whenever it can, even when that person isn't around—*especially* when that person isn't around to defend him or herself. It's easy to jump in and agree when someone's dirty laundry is aired behind their back, especially if we, too, have been hurt by that person. What if instead, we defended that person by jumping in with the benefit of the doubt? Usually there's a back story we don't know and the one "in question" is doing the best they know how at that moment, with cards in hand of which we are unaware. Wouldn't we want others to give *us* the benefit of the doubt and come to our defense when we're not around? It comes down to grace. Just as God's grace protects us, so are we to protect others with grace.

Love always trusts. This means believing the best in every person and situation. Love is not suspicious and doubting of the other person's character and motives without good reason. Love believes others are innocent until proven guilty, not the other way around. This does not mean we naïvely abandon all discernment. It means the benefit of the doubt is given before accusation; we don't rush to believe the worst. If a problem arises, love doesn't jump immediately to blame the other person. Not that trust does not need to be earned back once broken, but love hopes that trust can and will be restored, and gives it the opportunity to be earned back, even if with a guarded heart. It's not constantly singing the "Remember When You Broke My Heart Reprise." It's not gripping resentment, preventing trust from ever having a chance of being regained. Love always trusts, or hopes to trust, again.

Reflection: In what relationships do you feel you have not protected another the way you should have? How could you better support the character of your co-workers? Your spouse? Family members? Friends? Whom have you shut out from your heart due to broken trust? Could you give them opportunity to earn back your trust?

Prayer: Lord, thank you for teaching me what real love looks like. Help me to understand the responsibility you have placed on me to protect those you've put in my life. I pray I would always give grace when I don't have all the details. Help me, with healthy boundaries in place, to hope for repaired trust in my broken relationships. Amen.

Worship: "This Is Love" by Natalie Grant and "Surely We Can Change" by David Crowder Band

41

Hang on & Hope

It always protects, always trusts,
always hopes, always perseveres.
1 Corinthians 13:7

Love always hopes. Hope is the full anticipation that good will rise up. It keeps pushing through defeat to get to that ultimate success. Love does not dwell on past dead-ends but looks forward to the future with confidence and faith in God's ability. This is not a false sense of reality, but a resting on God's promise that he is working all things together for good. This hope knows God can move mountains and, also, trusts he has a better plan if he chooses to leave those mountains in place.

The opposite of this hope is pessimism. Think of a pessimist in your life who sees only the worst possible outcomes, notices only the flaws in people, does not explore options to overcome his or her circumstances, and complains of being stuck. These pessimists are even annoyed by others who see the bright side of things. They are killjoys, bringing out the worst in everyone. Now think of an optimist in your life who chooses to focus on the good, counts their blessings, encourages others, brings out the best in everyone, and explores ways to better situations. With which person would you rather spend a day? Which person is making strides toward making the world a better place? Which person do you want to be? It all starts with the way you view the world. A gloomy outlook does not thrive in a heart full of hope.

Love always perseveres. *Persevere* here means to take on the assault of an enemy without surrender. It is carrying a heavy load but refusing to let it defeat you. It means hanging in there when the going gets tough and people become hard to love. We tend to bail out when we've grown weary, the situation becomes complicated, or people become hard to love. Many times, if we don't like something petty that happens in a church, we go find another church. If we find things getting stale in the marriage, we look for the pizazz we crave elsewhere. A friend lets us down, so we discard the friendship. However, relationships become stronger when we climb from the valley back to the mountaintop together. Growing stronger together requires perseverance. It means we "take on the assault of the enemy without surrender" to reach that peak once again. Rich relationships forgive, stick it out, and work toward better days with fierce determination. When we say, "I'm not quitting. I'm here to stay," God often blesses us with something more beautiful than we originally had. Recall the rewards God gave when Abram and Sarai waited for a child and when Job stuck with God through his trials. It's through the climb, through persevering, we gain strength.

(Note: There are times friendships become toxic, crossing healthy boundaries, or marriages are corroded with abuse or adultery. These are not the instances where God is asking us to persevere. Please seek professional counsel if you are in one of these situations.)

Reflection: In what situations have you not held on to hope? Is there a relationship you gave up when you could have persevered? How could you have applied the truth concerning godly love, hope, and perseverance to those situations and relationships? Do you tend to be pessimistic about the future or hopeful for the best outcome, trusting God will create beauty from ashes?

Prayer: God of Hope, help me to look for the good in my situations and to anticipate the good in others. Give me the strength I need to persevere with fierce determination in the areas I'm lacking stick-to-it-iveness. Please lift my struggling relationships up from the valleys to the mountaintops. Amen.

Worship: "Life Is Good" by Courtnie Ramirez and "'Til The End" by Jeremy Camp

42

How the Christian Measures Up

Love never fails. But where there are prophecies, they will cease; where there are tongues, they will be stilled; where there is knowledge, it will pass away.

1 Corinthians 13:8

What makes a man or woman "godly"? What would you say is the standard of measurement for a truly spiritual person? The amount of money he gives? How often she goes to church? How many poor people she fed? How elaborate are his prayers? How many Scriptures she posted on social media? The Corinthian Church believed the measurement of spirituality was the demonstration of spiritual gifts. In fact, they were so busy assessing their lives by their spiritual gifts, they had forgotten about love. It's not an out-of-the-ordinary thought. I've been to some churches in this century who use spiritual gifts to determine if one is truly a believer. If that's not it, what is the gauge that registers some degree of godliness? Paul teaches us in 1 Corinthians 13 that gauge is love. Jesus taught us the same thing, "By this everyone will know that you are my disciples, if you love one another" (John 13:35). Love, pure and simple.

Loving well is the gold standard, not whether we sing well or teach well. Why is this? Why does God determine our spirituality by the way we love and not by the good deeds we've accomplished or the way we use our gifts? Paul answers this question clearly. It is because spiritual gifts are temporary; they will pass away. But love is enduring. Spiritual gifts are only a small part of the whole, while love is complete. Paul contrasts this God-rooted act—love—with the things that will not last, the things that do have an expiration date. The temporary spiritual gifts are designed to lead us to love, which never ends.

The gifts of knowledge, prophecy, and tongues are important God-given gifts with the purpose of growing the church. But they have a time and place, and that time and place has an end. They were never intended for eternity.

Love never fails. It is never ending. It doesn't accumulate in our hearts until we give it away, depleting our reservoir of love. It's doesn't operate as a filling and emptying. Many times, we don't even have it to give when we need to give it. When we're running on empty, if we simply ask God for this power we lack, he will always supply us with the power to love as he loves, but sometimes not until that very moment we need it.

Oftentimes, we feel we have nothing to give, certainly not the selfless, unconditional love God has called us to give. But he did not call us to a love we can't extend. If our hearts are willing and we ask, he will always empower us to love well. To say we can't extend love to the unlovable is to say God's love isn't enough.

There have been many times in my life I came to the end of my own abilities to act in a loving manner. I knew the exact point in time I had reached the end of my ability. Then, God's love kicked in and gave me supernatural self-control, kindness, and patience—all certainly outside my own capacity. The powerful stream of God's pure love carried me along. Love never fails.

As we get in the habit of realizing how powerless we are to love on our own, asking for a supply of God's love to give, dying to self, and living for loving others, we begin to find ease in this cycle. The more we practice giving love away, the more we show love effortlessly. Receiving from God and giving to others is a cycle that continues, becoming natural and habitual the longer we practice it. Love that never fails. There is a bottomless supply. We need only tap in.

Reflection: Have you ever put knowledge above love? What about teaching or exercising spiritual gifts? How can we lose focus of love when we're "doing things" for the Kingdom? Is there something that needs to change to prioritize love to the top where God has made it? Think of a time you realized you had no love to give on your own and then God clearly empowered you to love.

Prayer: Loving Father, my ability to love is so limited. Please provide me with the capacity to love beyond my own feelings and limited scope.

Continue to pour your fuel of love into me so I can demonstrate your supernatural love to all, even those who are difficult to love. May everyone know I am yours because I have loved well and may that love point them to you. Amen

---

Worship: "Nothing to Give" by 7eventh Time Down and "Fill Me With Your Love" by Robert Martin

43

The Distorted View

For we know in part and we prophesy in part, but when completeness comes, what is in part disappears. When I was a child, I talked like a child, I thought like a child, I reasoned like a child. When I became a man, I put the ways of childhood behind me. For now we see only a reflection as in a mirror; then we shall see face to face. Now I know in part; then I shall know fully, even as I am fully known.

1 Corinthians 13:9-12

"For we know in part and we prophesy is part, but...what is in part disappears," we are told in 1 Corinthians 13:9-10. This can be confusing. What is it that is "in part" and will be disappearing? The "in part" is referring to spiritual gifts of knowledge and prophecy—knowledge of God and Scripture. Do you find God and his ways difficult to understand? We are given only bits and pieces revealing the mysteries of God. Not one person gets the whole. We must depend on coming together to piece parts of the puzzle in a shared experience to understand the mysteries of God. Even then, though the picture becomes broader, we still have only a distorted image.

Paul says, "For now we see only a reflection as in a mirror; then we shall see face to face." At the time this was written, mirrors were made of polished steel or other metals. They weren't like the clear images we see in the mirrors of today. The metal mirrors distorted the image. So, when Paul says we will "see face to face," he is saying we will see the fine details much more clearly. We will see God without the distortions and imperfections cause by our clouded vision.

I think we can all agree, looking at other Christians gives us a distorted view of Christ. Even in reading the Bible, we are only given a small glimpse of who he is. Our finite minds can't fully fathom the depths of the infinite God. We see

Jesus now in a dim, unclear way, but one day that barrier will fall, the mist will fade, and we will see him with perfect clarity.

God won't always remain a mystery! We are given hope in verse 10, that one day, the partial will pass away and will be replaced by the whole, fully knowing God as he fully knows us. What a day that will be! Mysteries revealed! Confusion washed away! Our minds blown by the knowledge of God!

We can try to gain knowledge and, in fact, are called to do so (2 Peter 3:18, Ephesians 1:17), but one day, our spiritual gifts of prophecy and knowledge will become obsolete, and do you know what we'll be asked? We'll be asked, "Did you love?"

Reflection: What are some questions you have about God that have yet to be answered? Do these unanswered questions cause your faith to waiver? Or do you stand strong with anticipation of knowing the answers one day?

Prayer: God, life is confusing, and I have so many questions about you. Your ways are so different than my ways and my human mind cannot understand. I look forward to the day your mysteries are unscrambled, and light is shed on them. I can't wait to see you completely undistorted! Please help me to know you better and empower me to be faithful to you, in spite of all I don't know or understand. Until then, help me to love well. Amen.

Worship: "Someday" by Nichole Nordeman, "As Long As I'm Here" by Brandon Heath, and "All That Lives Forever" by Steffany Gretzinger

44

Faith, Hope & Love

And now these three remain: faith, hope, and love. But the greatest of these is love.

1 Corinthians 13:13

Of all God's gifts, love is the greatest. It's the cut above, the ace that takes the cake. It upstages and outshines all qualities, even hope and faith! Why is that?

Let's review faith. Faith is an active belief and trust in what we do not see. "Can you see God? You haven't seen him? I've never seen the wind. I see the effects of the wind, but I've never seen the wind. There's a mystery to it," says Billy Graham.[5] And so it is with God. He is a mystery, yet we see his fingerprints all around us through his creation, his light in the darkness, and his interventions in our lives. We must have faith to believe in this God we don't see with our eyes. In order to unquestionably obey him, we need a pretty substantial supply of it. If we need a greater supply of faith, we simply ask for more and the Giver of Faith will not withhold from us (Ephesians 2:8, 1 Corinthians 12:7-11, Acts 3:16 Romans 12:3, Mark 11:24).

Faith is not simply a thought or belief. Beliefs don't become "faith" until we make decisions and plan our actions based on those beliefs. Faith strengthens our ambition and keeps us moving forward, without fear. Faith allows us to say with Shadrach, Meshach, and Abednego, "If we are thrown into the blazing furnace, the God we serve is able to deliver us from it, and he will deliver us from Your Majesty's hand. But even if he does not, we want you to know, Your Majesty, that we will not serve your gods or worship the image of gold you have set up," (Daniel 3:17-18). This is God-given faith in the face of the unknown. Faith motivates us to move forward, even when everything else is pushing us backward, allowing us to achieve great things.

In reviewing hope, we learn it's the feeling that what is desired is, in fact, attainable. Hope is what keeps us going when the task seems impossible. For the single mom, barely hanging on by a thread, hope is what keeps her from throwing in the towel. If she believes God is able and help is in her near future, she can take one more day. Hope for a healthy marriage keeps couples fighting for it. Hope is a gift from God to help us persevere through hard times so we can experience the benefit when we rise out of the muck. "...but those who hope in the LORD will renew their strength. They will soar on wings like eagles; they will run and not grow weary, they will walk and not be faint" (Isaiah 40:31).

Hope is similar to faith in that it, also, spurs us to press forward despite the fiery furnace that threatens us. Though we are often taking steps in the dark, we are not asked to have a completely blind hope or faith. We have been given fulfilled prophecies, miracles, and stories of those who took blind steps successfully. These accounts put steel in our bones. He has kept all other promises throughout all time. He won't stop now.

And now for the crown jewel, "the greatest of these"—love. We discussed agape love (the word used for love in 1 Corinthians 13) thoroughly the past few devotions as we've been studying and growing from this chapter. Why does the chapter conclude with the notion that love is the greatest attribute of them all? Faith and hope are considerably important as they keep us moving despite trials around us. However, they both serve only the person to whom they belong. Love, however, serves *others*, and that's what Jesus is all about! Genuine love points to Jesus and is our greatest calling (Matt 22:36-40). His astounding love saves and transforms us to reflect him because God *is* love. We are never more like Jesus than when we love. And sometimes loving others helps them hold on to their hope and faith. Maybe that is why it is the greatest of all.

Reflection: Have you ever experienced or witnessed an event that made you pause and think, *That has to be God; there's no other way that just happened?* Who in your life demonstrates incredible faith? What hopes are you holding on to right now that keep you going? In what ways can showing agape love to others help them hold onto their faith and hope?

Prayer: God, thank you for the faith and hope you provide to me that helps me keep going through [name the trials you're going through]. Show me ways I can demonstrate agape love in all circumstances to those around me, so they have a little more wind in their sails to persevere through their trials. Help me to take seriously what you have deemed the greatest calling on earth—to love. Please strengthen my faith when I feel I'm walking in the dark, and may my hope always be in you. Amen.

Worship: "I Wait" by All Sons & Daughters, "My Hope Is In You" by Aaron Shust, and "Love" by Chris Tomlin

45

Known & Fully Loved

For you created my inmost being; you knit me together in my mother's womb. I praise you because I am fearfully and wonderfully made; your works are wonderful. I know that full well. My frame was not hidden from you when I was made in the secret place, when I was woven together in the depths of the earth. Your eyes saw my unformed body; all the days ordained for me were written in your book before one of them came to be. How precious to me are your thoughts, God! How vast is the sum of them! Were I to count them, they would outnumber the grains of sand— when I awake, I am still with you.

Psalm 139:13-18

Do you ever feel like your prayers are lost in space among a billion other prayers? You feel you're not heard? Maybe you think God has forgotten you or is "out to get you." Sometimes we dedicate time to spend with God and let our thoughts linger on him. Other times we're so busy, we only think about him from time to time. No matter how often we think of God, we may wonder, *Does God ever think about me as well?* These verses promise us that he does, indeed! He formed us in the darkness of the womb, he sees our days before they even come about, and his thoughts concerning us outnumber the grains of sand. Stop and think about that. Have you been to the beach? Could you count the grains of sand in a bucket? How about the sand covering the entire earth? Impossible! Yet this is the number outweighed by the thoughts of God about you! Therefore, he thinks about you more than you think about him!

He created us, knit us together in our mothers' wombs, not just our physical bodies, but our personalities, characteristics, emotions, and mental makeup. Each of us are exactly what we were created to be. Every aspect of us created with intention.

Verse 14 says, "I am fearfully and wonderfully made…" "Fear" is a negative emotion. It is the idea or sense that something bad, or harmful, is about to happen. But we were fearfully and wonderfully made, so what does "fearfully" here mean? The word *fearfully* is derived from the root *yara*, which expresses a reverent awe. It is mind blowing that the God who created us is in astonishment at his own work and even *admires* us.

No one better knows us than our Creator. God knows our every thought, every habit, every action we've ever done and will do! Even then, after knowing our depths, he is still in awe of us. If God is in awe over us, should we not accept ourselves as the treasure God knows we are? Should we not live by the way God views us? Instead, we feel worthless and live as if we are trash, allowing our warped sense of worth to affect the way we treat ourselves and those around us, leading to our own demise. It is a journey to fully embrace God's love and acceptance—to move the knowledge that we are cherished treasures from our heads into our hearts, and then into our actions, to live like we're loved and accepted.

We often hear, "God loves you," but when things are falling apart around us, it's hard to feel the truth of that. It's especially hard when we're not spending quality time with him. Often, he speaks his love to us when we spend quiet time listening. So, we've got to take the time to meditate on the Word and ask the Spirit to plant it in our hearts.

It is a joy to know God thinks about us, that he hasn't forgotten about us. When we feel like things are falling apart, and question his presence, we can remind ourselves his thoughts on us persist and outnumber the grains of sand. He continues to oversee our lives. His thoughts, his plans, and his ways are beyond our imagination. We pursue knowing him and his ways, but even our best knowledge of him falls greatly short of understanding him. Though we don't have the capacity to fully know and understand God, we can rest assured he fully knows and understands us, thinks about us, and loves us.

Reflection: Is it hard for you to believe God thinks about you? How would your life be different if you came to truly believe that he treasures you and his thoughts of you are unceasing and innumerable?

Prayer: God, thank you that your thoughts are on me. Although sometimes it feels I was simply created and then forgotten, I've learned your thoughts persist on me. Please give me a new perspective on my worth, *your* perspective on my worth, and may it change me, the way I live, and the way I treat others. Amen.

Worship: "Not Forgotten" by Israel Houghton and "Who I Am" by Blanca

46

All Are Precious

For you created my inmost being; you knit me together in my mother's womb. I praise you because I am fearfully and wonderfully made; your works are wonderful. I know that full well. My frame was not hidden from you when I was made in the secret place, when I was woven together in the depths of the earth. Your eyes saw my unformed body; all the days ordained for me were written in your book before one of them came to be. How precious to me are your thoughts, God! How vast is the sum of them! Were I to count them, they would outnumber the grains of sand— when I awake, I am still with you.

Psalm 139:13-18

Yes, you astonish the Creator. And so does your boss, your co-worker, your mother-in-law, your brother. You are not the only person who was created with awe and who astonishes God. Every person around you amazes their Creator. Therefore, we need to see others in light of that truth. Every time you look down on someone, you are mentally belittling someone who impresses God. Every time you insult someone, you are insulting someone who blows God's mind. Every time you hold a grudge against someone, you are holding a grudge against someone whom God cherishes. When you deny the worth of another person, it offends God.

How would it look to view every person in the world as a precious child of God? What if we saw all of humanity as a beloved brother or sister? We would listen a whole lot more. Rather than shutting down one another's thoughts and opinions to get them to see our own, we would show respect and take their views into consideration. There would be less screaming, fewer insults, less condescension, less exclusion, and less neglect. There would be more respect and acceptance. We would understand full well we have not walked a mile in another's shoes, and we would stop judging.

It is a journey to get to the place where we can love and accept ourselves. An even greater journey to love and accept those who bring out the worst in us. Our responsibility is to love others—everyone. We don't get to decide if they are worthy of our love. God already decided they are.

Reflection: Who are the top three hardest people in your life to love? Think of one good quality they each possess. If you fully understood God's love for them, how would it change the way you treated them?

Prayer: Loving God, Creator of All, help me to see others the way you see them, and to love them the way you love them. My understanding is so limited, it's hard for me to grasp the deep love you have for those I find hard to love. Help me to see what it is in them that you love. Teach me to be a vessel of your love to them. Amen.

Worship: "Kings & Queens" by Audio Adrenaline and "Give Me Your Eyes" by Brandon Heath

47

Plans—Hold Them Loose, Hold Them Tight

Commit your actions to the L*ORD, and your plans will succeed.*

Proverbs 16:3 NLT

We all make plans for our lives whether it be for our career, a vacation, our retirement, or simply a night out. Some of us put a lot of time and effort into carefully researching, asking for advice, and planning out all the details, while others of us fly by the seat of our pants and hope for the best. No matter our style, we all want the same outcome: for our plans to succeed. Solomon says if you want your plans to succeed, "commit your actions to the Lord." But what exactly does he mean by that? How do we commit our actions to the Lord?

Committing our actions to the Lord means surrendering our plans to his will. It means we seek him first with an awareness that our plans may need to change and a willingness to give up what *we* want to do in exchange for what *God* wants us to do. It's in this place we'll find those plans he's had for us since before the beginning of time (Ephesians 2:10), and it's here we'll find soul satisfying success.

How do we know God's will? It's found in his Word. When our plans require dishonesty or immorality, are clearly going against Scripture, or are not beneficial for our families, then we demolish those plans and ask for guidance toward another plan. Parting with a plan that is not in God's will is one aspect of committing our actions to the Lord. We recognize we cannot be led by greed or what "feels right" in our own eyes, but instead, by the Word of God.

Another aspect of committing our actions to the Lord is sticking to a God-given plan when the going gets tough. Many times, we question God's will because the door seems closed, or the path becomes too difficult. Keep in mind,

God gave Moses a plan in a burning bush (Exodus 3). Nothing could have been clearer than that! God's plan: Moses was to approach Pharoah to request freedom for the Israelites. Moses followed through but it wasn't until the door slammed shut nine times—nine plagues later— that Pharoah finally relented and let God's people go.

Satan wants us to fall flat on our faces. He hates when we follow God's path, and he throws every dart our way to throw us off that path. When the going gets tough, it is tempting to second-guess, change course, or even abandon ship from the God-given plans, like a marriage, a mission, consistency in disciplining children, giving to a friend in need, a sacrifice God requested, or maintaining integrity on the job. When we're plodding through the valley, we can't call into question what God said on the mountain. We need to hang on tight to what God told us, then lean in to the promise from the one who wants us to succeed, the promise that he will give us renewed strength to keep going (Isaiah 40:31).

It makes sense to commit our plans to the one who is beyond the limits of time and space and filled with infinite knowledge and wisdom, to the one whose thoughts are higher than our thoughts and whose ways are higher than our ways (Isaiah 55:8-9). He not only sees the big picture that is unavailable to us, but also cares for and loves us with unimaginable depth. We may not always understand or agree with the plans he has for us, but we can trust he works all things for the good of those who love him, who have been called according to his purpose (Romans 8:28).

Go ahead and make your plans. If the plans came from your own heart, hold on to them loosely, willing to let go if God asks. If the plans came from the heart of God, when the storm comes, remember that vision and hang on tight.

Reflection: Think about some current plans you have. If God changed your plans, how would that set with you? Are you open to considering a change in plans if God made that clear to you? What are you currently pursuing that you're certain is God's will? In what way have you experienced success after facing storms and persevering?

Prayer: Sovereign God, thank you for giving my life purpose and planning great things for me. I realize I am not in control. I'm placing my plans under your authority. Help me to let go of plans that are clearly not your plans. Please make your will clear to me and give me a receptive heart. When you have plans for me, give me the perseverance to press through when the going gets tough. Amen.

Worship: "I'm Letting Go" by Francesca Battistelli and "Carry On" by Tauren Wells

48

Feeling Betrayed but Won't Be Swayed

Commit your actions to the LORD, and your plans will succeed.

PROVERBS 16:3 NLT

Sometimes, we make plans and commit them to God, but they still don't succeed. Not the way we expected. Early in our marriage, my husband, Joel, was working on his apprenticeship under a dishonest supervisor. He didn't realize his boss was shady at first, but eventually it became clear when Joel was asked to sneak deceptive information into his work. Refusing to take that route, he became the joke of the office and acquired the nickname "Conserva-Joel." At Christmastime, he was let go. "Conserva-Joel" was broadsided and wondered where God was in all this. He was doing what he knew to be right in God's eyes but was punished instead of given the success he thought God gave to those who commit their actions to him.

When I was thirty-five, I had just finished my bachelor's degree with the premed classes I needed for admission to grad school. I was in unswerving pursuit of my dream of becoming a Physician Assistant. I had three kids at the time, worked in a hospital, and had been taking pre-requisite classes part-time for seven years. I had worked diligently to attain and "A" in every class, knowing I needed that edge to get into such a competitive program. It imposed an incredible amount of stress and required many sacrifices to get to that point. It was a long time coming! And it was then, while applying to PA programs across the country, I was diagnosed with an incurable cancer, turning my life upside-down. My plans to become a PA were left in ruins. My plan, instead, became to seek out how I might stay alive. The questions went from, *Which school will I attend?* to *Will I see my children graduate high school?* I was devastated. Over the next several months, invitations trickled in for me to interview for PA programs all over the country, and each time, it felt like a punch in my gut. I had been working for years toward that goal! After all the studying, the writing, the exams, the classrooms, the assignments, and the clinicals, only to see it all dissolve into a heap of what could have been, left me feeling dismayed.

Sometimes, we're left dazed by an abrupt change in plans after we're knocked off the course which we had been certain God wanted us. It's during those moments we question God's provision, his compassion, and sometimes even his existence. Those are the times God shows up and says, "First, take this step." Then later, he illuminates just one more step. Eventually, we find he's leading us to success one slow step at a time on a curvy, bumpy road. We must hang on tight to him with patience in expectation, sometimes waiting far longer than we anticipate, but he always comes through.

"Conserva-Joel" found an internship with a new supervisor, a man who values integrity and is a leader in the top of his field. This man trained "Conserva-Joel" to be one of the best as well. God led me to cancer treatments that have had minimal side effects. I'm healthier than I have ever been, and I just watched my first son graduate. My career aspirations were crushed, but I can look back at all the ways God showed himself strong, provided for me in ways I couldn't have dreamt, strengthened my faith, and taught me things that can't be learned from a book. I wouldn't go back and change that cancer diagnosis if I had the power to do so. In both Joel's and my situations, it required surrender of *our* plans and leaning in to *God's* plan. God had something better in mind for each of us.

If you're feeling betrayed and dismayed, take courage and hang on tight. Something better is on the way!

Reflection: Think of a time you experienced a devastating change in plans. How were you able to see God's hand in it? Have you ever felt betrayed by the promises of God? In what ways did you see success where the world may have seen failure? What change in plans is currently leaving you feeling betrayed? Ask God to strengthen your faith in his promise to lead you to success when you commit your actions to him.

Prayer: God, I know you're in control and your plans for me are good. Please forgive me for the times I have doubted that. Remind me that your plans are always good, your ways are higher than my ways and your thoughts are higher than my thoughts. Help me to hang on tight to you when I feel betrayed and to remember something better is coming. Amen.

Worship: "Let It Rain (Is There Anybody)" by Crowder and "Thy Will" by Hillary Scott

49

The Healing Power of Pleasant Words

Pleasant words are a honeycomb, sweet to
the soul and healing to the bones.

PROVERBS 16:24 NASB

Words have incredible power—the power to make or break a relationship, a business, a family, a church, a marriage, and especially impressionable children. With just our words alone, we have the power to cause another to give up his dreams or to pursue them. We can cause a child to doubt herself by creating fear and apprehension, or we can give her the confidence to boldly lead those around her. We can cause our friends and spouse to give up in defeat or inspire them to accomplish what feels impossible.

Honey is both sweet and healing, as are our pleasant words to others. There have been times in my life, I felt as if I were failing but the words of another kept me going. Once in particular, I was going through a parenting rough patch. My kids' choices didn't reflect the way I raised them, and I felt defeat. Every day I'd wake up and wonder where I went wrong. I would listen to Satan's lies telling me I was a failure of a mother. It was at that time, a friend wrote me, out of the blue, telling me she thought I was a great mama. She said she could tell I had made many sacrifices for my children and had spent time training them right. She said she was impressed by the number of sacrifices I had made for them. I can't tell you how sweet those words were to my soul, how healing to my weary bones!

When we've had a bad day, to whom do we run? Definitely not to the ones whose words have so often deflated our ideas, judged us, or wounded us. We run to the ones whose words are life-giving, "sweet to the soul and healing to the bones."

Self-evaluation time: *Do others run to me when they have a problem? Do my words convey understanding and cause others to move toward healing? Do I criticize people, further wounding them? Have my words contributed to others' confidence?*

If we are critical by nature and generally short on "pleasant words," we need to recalibrate and take time to notice something valuable, good, or beautiful in others. Some people make it hard to see the good in them, but if we ask God to help us see what he sees in them (I can assure you, it is something beautiful), he will gladly open our eyes to things we never saw and give us the right words to give them a new spring in their step. When we let them know the good we see in them, who knows what kind of rockstars we will unleash!

Reflection: Think of a time someone spoke sweet words to you in a moment you needed them. Whom do you know could benefit from your healing words today? Take the time to write it out, text it, or verbalize it to them.

Prayer: God, thank you for the encouragement of others that keeps me going when I feel defeated. I pray I would be sensitive to the way others are feeling and give them the right words in the right moments to heal their weary bones. Amen.

Worship: "Speak Life" by TobyMac and "Help Somebody" by Deitrick Haddon

50

A Spoonful of Sugar

Pleasant words are a honeycomb, sweet to
the soul and healing to the bones.

Proverbs 16:24 NASB

Election time is coming! What feelings do those words evoke in you? For most of us, it's anxiety as we're bombarded with the slanderous statements made by each candidate and their followers against those they oppose. The air is heavy with verbal assault, hatred, mudslinging, and slaughtering of reputations. It's just plain ugly. Where there once were fun-loving friendships, at election time, becomes friction and division.

If our words are hateful against a political side, odds are, the people we batter with our endless opinions have stopped listening to us anyway. Then we're just "preaching" to friends who already agree with us. Division accomplished.

So, do we just remain silent about issues that are important to us? Not necessarily. Mary Poppins enlightens us with wise advice, "Just a spoonful of sugar helps the medicine go down." The medicine (our words) has power, but the sugar (sweet words) makes it easier to swallow. Kind, gracious words accomplish far more than words spit out from a hateful heart. While angry words cause others' defenses to escalate, calm tones and words like, "I hear what you're saying, I respect your opinion, I can see why you think that… but I think…," go miles further.

The same is true for issues in other areas of our lives, within our families, our workplaces, and in the community. How about we make sure we're sweetening the medicine we want to go down? Let's pause before pouncing. Let's choose to hold that mighty tongue until emotions simmer down. Let's pray before we speak and ask for the necessary measure of sweet honey. It's possible for fights and subsequent deep wounds to be prevented. Holding the tongue is easier than attempting to repair a relationship after the damage is done.

To take it further than prevention, let's be proactive and intentional about offering encouragement, support, good cheer, inspiration, and hope to others. Let's start with our spouse and children, move on to the extended family, then spread it to social media and even to the strangers we run into. We never know just how badly someone needs to hear words "sweet to the soul" until we speak the "pleasant words" and watch their posture, life, and face brighten.

Reflection: When was the last time you had to make amends because of hurtful words you said? Would it have been better if you had held your tongue instead? How would your life change if someone was willing to give you just a little dose of encouragement every morning as you began your day? Consider doing this for those in your home, at work, within your extended family and even to strangers.

Prayer: Father, make my words sweet like honey. Take away my desire to lash out when I disagree or have been hurt. May I give pause to my angry thoughts and respond only after I've taken it to you and my anger has cooled. Give me your eyes to see the good in others and the courage to speak up with words of encouragement for them. Amen.

Worship: "The Comment Section" by Sidewalk Prophets and "Make Me Over" by Natalie Grant

51

The Environment for Sweet Honey

Pleasant words are a honeycomb, sweet to the soul and healing to the bones.

Proverbs 16:24 nasb

Beekeepers know the flavor of the honey depends on which kind of nectar the bees are consuming. The beekeepers strategically place the beehive near clover for the sweetest honey, near buckwheat for more antioxidants, and near alfalfa for a milder flavor. And so it goes with people, where we place ourselves matters. When we're in a field of negativity—consuming the nectar of doubt, cynicism, apathy, and pessimism—that acrid flavor is passed on to us, and out of us. However, when we're consuming the nectar from a sweet field, we will drip words that encourage and heal.

Friends are very influential in our lives. There is a saying, "Show me your friends and I'll show you your future." It's no surprise we become like the people we hang with. They shape the way we view the world, bend us in the direction of either pessimism or optimism, influence our passions, and direct us toward or away from certain paths. The Bible says this, "Walk with the wise and become wise, for a companion of fools suffers harm" (Proverbs 13:20). When we surround ourselves with life-giving, hope-inducing, faith-filled people, we will then exude life, hope, and faith to those around us as well.

Another environment of great influence is the media. There is evidence that watching the news increases anxiety and depression. If you are one who consumes the news for much of the day, try checking in just once a day. If you often listen to talk radio, try limiting it, especially the talk shows that tend to hype news and intensify worry. Listen to the news to gain information for the purpose of knowing how to work toward a brighter future instead of listening to the news with the attitude of grumbling and complaining about the direction the world is headed. Most importantly, pray when you watch the news. Prayer makes a difference in both the world and your anxiety. In 2 Chronicles 7:14, we read: "If my people, who are called by my name, will humble themselves and pray and seek my face and turn from their wicked ways, then I will hear from heaven, and I will forgive their sin and will heal their land." There aren't words sweeter to the soul and more healing to the bones than prayer.

Music stimulates the part of the brain that affects behavior and mood. What kinds of lyrical messages are we putting into our minds that are, in turn, affecting the way we think and live? I looked up the Billboard Top Ten songs as of this writing today. Here are some of the messages in those songs: *I'm better than you. I [crass action] your [crass word for a person]. I'm falling apart because you left me. I want to die. I'm not good enough. You're not good enough.* These songs give us images that rob us of the peace God wants us to have. Imagine the feelings we would have about ourselves, others, and life in general if we filled our heads with these songs day after day. What words would flow from us if we were consuming the nectar of today's most popular songs?

On the other hand, here are some of the messages of today's top ten worship songs: *I am held. I am loved. There is hope. God healed my heart. God will provide. I want to please God. I'm alive in Christ. God can do the impossible. I have nothing to be afraid of. God has the victory. God is faithful to me. God calls me friend. God turns my mourning to dancing.* What a stark contrast! Imagine the words of encouragement that would automatically flow from a heart filled with these life-giving words!

And where do these worship songs come from? Let's turn to the source of them, the Word of God, to renew our minds daily. God's words to us are encouraging, full of love and hope. Remember, what we are filled with is what we ooze onto others.

When we're deliberate about where we buzz—from the people we hang out with, to the news we fill our minds with, the music streaming into our hearts, and the Word of God we're reading—we can be sure the words that flow from our mouths will be sweet to others' souls and healing to their bones.

Reflection: In what kind of environment have you been buzzing around? What can you do to ensure you're buzzing in an environment of sweet nectar that produces sweet words? Do you need to spend more time with loving, faith-filled people? How much news are you watching or listening to daily? What messages do your favorite songs convey? How could you get more encouragement from the Word into your day?

Prayer: Most High God, I pray I would be more deliberate about the environment I "buzz" in and the "nectar" I am consuming. Help me to fill myself with the thoughts and ideas that produce the sweet honey of encouragement to those around me. Help me to fall in love with, and come to depend on, your Word so much that I would run to it daily. May I be one who brightens others and brings healing to their bones because I have taken these steps to consume sweet nectar. Amen.

Worship: "Make Me A River" by Casting Crowns, "The Peace of Christ" by Tommy Walker, and "Here As in Heaven" by Kari Jobe

52

Wars Cease

Be still and know that I am God.
Psalm 46:10

Be still and know that I am God," is a popular verse familiar for many. We see it on the walls of homes, on coffee mugs, and bracelets. What we might not know, though, is that it was written regarding wars. Let's read a few verses surrounding it to give us a bit more insight. "Come and see what the Lord has done, the desolations he has brought on the earth. He makes wars cease to the ends of the earth. He breaks the bow and shatters the spear; he burns the shields with fire. He says, 'Be still, and know that I am God; I will be exalted among the nations, I will be exalted in the earth'" (v. 8-10). When we see it in its entire context, we see God telling his battle-weary people to snap out of their fear, refocus their attention on who he is, and to be in *awe* of what he can do!

If he could make wars on earth cease, surely, he can make the wars in our hearts cease! Our daily battles may pale in comparison to war and its catastrophic impact, yet we may *feel* we are being annihilated just the same. Battles become a war that make us feel as though the very ground beneath us is shaking (as described in Psalm 46:2-3). We lose a job, experience our marriage dissolving, receive a devastating diagnosis, watch our children suffer, or lose a loved one. Indeed, these battles can feel as heavy on our hearts as if we were standing in a literal war zone. We are battle weary.

Is evil winning while God remains silent? Sometimes it feels that way. Our understanding is so limited. We have on blinders and are unable to see the big picture of every situation—past, present, and future. We don't always understand that our trials come with a purpose. It seems completely unlikely, in our tethered minds, that *good* dare come out of our situation. However, we can know with absolute certainty that God is with us, stretching out his hand to help us. The God who brings chaos into order and peace out of conflict is right there with us, waiting to intervene—waiting for our request to step into our desolations and "shatter the spear."

Reflection: What "wars" are you currently fighting? Are you able to see God's hand in the battle, or do you only hear silence? What encourages you in the verses surrounding Psalm 46:10? Can you believe the truths here? If you want to believe these truths but are not yet there, pray with the broken-hearted father of Mark 9:24, "I do believe; help me overcome my unbelief!" and wait for the bow to be broken.

Prayer: God, I am battle weary. I know you have the power to stop wars. I pray you will stop this war in my life that's burdening my heart. Help me to search for the good you have in store. I anxiously await to see your hand in my situation. I'm looking forward to seeing what you will do! Amen.

Worship: "Fight For You" by Jason Gray and "Tonight" by Francesca Battistelli

53

Surrender

Be still and know that I am God.

Psalm 46:10

I once had a foster daughter who was hiding an infected wound on her hand. Past experience taught her adults could not be trusted. Afraid of the pain it might cause if she asked me take care of it, she went to great lengths to hide it from me. It wasn't until a week later, I was helping her put on her gloves when I noticed. It was pus-filled and needed a small hole poked through the dead skin to allow the pressure to escape. Having many anxieties over the multitude of *other* things out of her control, her behavior over this minor situation was blown way out of proportion. After an hour of coaxing her to let me gently poke the needle through to release the pressure, there was no letting up from her. The screaming and kicking continued relentlessly. When I finally was able to get the needle through, she had been so busy in her tantrum, she didn't even notice it was done. When I pointed out it was finished, she immediately straightened up and said in her cheery voice, "Oh! That wasn't so bad."

The gentle poke of the needle brought her relief. But she needed to first stop hiding her pain, hoping it would go away on its own and second, to be still long enough for me to take care of the "impurity" in her.

God asks us to hand over the reins, to stop freaking out, and to be still long enough to let him help us. When we're kicking and flailing about in our fear and pain, he is longing for us to "be still" and "know" him as our rescuer. He tells us to lay down our weapons and trust him for the victory—to trust his timing is perfect, his ways are perfect, and his plan is perfect.

Many times, "Be still and know that I am God," gets shortened to "Be still and know." The psychology of the world tells us to take time to develop inner serenity. While inner serenity is good, the Bible says we achieve stillness by *knowing God* personally. When we know him, we understand his heart and comprehend that he is loving, gracious, and redeeming. We learn he is trustworthy, which leads us to surrender ourselves unquestionably.

During our wars, we are given a choice. We can freak out, fight, and struggle on the front lines, hoping God has our backs when we go down, or we can be still and know that God has a perfect plan and is already there in the trenches. We can believe we are the center of our own universe and advise God how and when to help us, or we can realize who is who. *Being still and knowing that he is God* gives us clear perspective on who is the commanding officer.

This psalm is the instruction to overpower our *fear* with *faith*. During our war, God says the peace that comes from knowing him is enough to overcome—even though the earth around us threatens to fall apart (verses 1-3). The people in this psalm heard the command to "be still and know" who is God and found God blew their imaginations!

Reflection: What do you tend to "freak out" over? How can you shift your perspective as to who is in control? Though your circumstance may not change, how could this psalm change your perspective of your circumstance?

Prayer: God, you are the Great I AM. Sometimes I forget you are at the center of it all. Sometimes in my mind, I am the lone ranger. I lose focus of who I really am and who you are. Help me to stop fighting. I lay my weapon down and trust you to take care of my battles. God, blow my mind with what you can do when I release the control I hold so tightly. Amen.

Worship: "Giving You All Control" by Jeremy Camp, "White Flag" by Chris Tomlin and "The Father's Song" by Upperroom

54

The Radiant Son

The Son is the radiance of God's glory and the exact representation of his being, sustaining all things by his powerful word. After he had provided purification for sins, he sat down at the right hand of the Majesty in heaven.

Hebrews 1:3

Why is space "dark" when the sun is in space? It appears dark to us, and speckled with "little" bright stars, but since the sun is out there, we know that isn't true. Let's dive into a little physics lesson. Light travels in a straight line unless it reflects off something or is bent by a lens. We can see the red dot of a laser pointer because it reflects off the object it hits, but we can't actually see the beam of the laser unless it reflects off dust or fog particles in the air. So, even though the sun is in space, filling it with light, the space appears black *unless* we are looking at something that reflects that light.

The word *radiance* in Greek is *apaugasma* and is translated by Thayer's Greek Lexicon as "reflected brightness."[6] Scripture says Jesus is the "reflected brightness" of God's glory. Though we don't see God the Father, we see his reflection in Jesus. When we see Jesus, we see God the Father. Jesus said, in John 1:18, "No one has ever seen God, but the one and only Son, who is himself God and is in closest relationship with the Father, has made him known." The Greek word for "made him known" is *exegeomai*, which means to tell, to lead forward and out, or to make known a teaching. Jesus makes known the detailed information of the glory of the Father. If we desire to understand God and his plan for humanity, we must look to Jesus.

Some of us view God, the Father, as angry, violent, dangerous, and even hateful in his harsh dealings with people. On the other hand, we view Jesus as compassionate, loving, and merciful. In our topic verse today, we read Jesus is the exact representation of the Father. This bewilders us if we read only segments of the Old Testament. When we read the entire Old Testament as a whole, we see God's mercy, compassion, and readiness to redeem anyone who turns from his evil ways. Those harsh dealings, aside from the big picture, become a stumbling block for those who want to know God as loving and compassionate. With Jesus as the reflection of God, we have assurance God does not aim to obliterate us but to join us in our suffering, to serve us, to redeem us, and have relationship eternally with us. Though God has the ability to demolish and devastate, his willingness to redeem is great. He went to the point of painstaking suffering to prove it. The Old Testament's portrayal of God's anger toward sin teaches us God hates sin. He doesn't hate *us*. He hates sin. If we can understand the depth of his hatred for sin, we can realize the depth of his mercy to redeem our sinful selves by his own suffering.

Reflection: Have you struggled to view God as loving? How does the idea of Jesus being the reflection of God change your view of God? How can you follow Jesus's example and be the "radiance" of God's glory to the world?

Prayer: God, forgive me for sometimes viewing you as an angry God out to destroy us sinners. When I look to your "reflection," I see who you truly are—loving, forgiving, compassionate and yearning for relationship with me. God, I accept your sacrifice and embrace your mercy. Help me to follow Jesus's example and reflect you in this dark world. Amen.

Worship: "See His Love" by Jesus Culture and "Stars" by David Crowder Band

55

The Sustaining Son

The Son is the radiance of God's glory and the exact representation of his being, sustaining all things by his powerful word. After he had provided purification for sins, he sat down at the right hand of the Majesty in heaven.

HEBREWS 1:3

Scientists measured both the amount of mass in the universe and the gravitational force that holds galaxies and solar systems together. What they discovered is that there is not nearly enough gravitational effect to hold all the known matter together. Scientists are in wonder and asking what force is holding all this mass together? They refer to this unknown force as "dark energy." *A New York Times* editorial states, "But observing dark matter and knowing what it is are very different, and we are nowhere near the latter. Then, beyond the problem of dark matter lies the greater problem of dark energy. This is a mysterious universe and the more we know about it, the more mysterious it seems."[7] Basically, the world doesn't have a clue how this universe is being held together.

Hebrews says it is Jesus "sustaining all things by his powerful word." According to the Bible, we live in a created universe upheld by none other than Jesus himself. His spoken word caused all things to come into being and his word sustains that being even today. Contrary to popular belief, we are not living in a chaotic accident.

The word *sustaining* is active, not passive, meaning Jesus did not set up our world and then walk away. Though it sometimes feels he just left it to fall apart, the form of the verb infers he is actively involved with his creation. "For from him and through him and for him are all things" (Romans 11:36). By him all things were created (past), through him all things are being sustained (present), and for him all things are to be reconciled (future). The One who created the perfect earth, and originally innocent humanity, is the one who will make a new earth and redeem fallen humanity (Isaiah 65:17).

Jesus sustains the universe, and Jesus sustains you. American soldiers, during the Vietnam War, referred to a specific nut on a helicopter as a "Jesus nut." This nut held the main rotor to the mast of the helicopter. If the "Jesus nut" were to fail in flight, the helicopter would detach from the rotor, crash, and burn. When you feel your life is crashing and burning, remember Jesus holds all things together—the universe and your life. Go to him. Listen as he directs your path (Proverbs 3:6). Allow him to hold you (Psalm 139:10). Allow him to sustain you.

Reflection: When you understand how small you are in relation to the universe, is it hard to believe you are significant to the Creator of it all? Is there any area of life where you feel you are crashing and burning? How can you take the knowledge that Jesus sustains all and apply it to your own life circumstances? Commit to trusting Jesus to uphold you and make a way.

Prayer: Sustainer of the Universe, it's hard to comprehend the magnitude of this universe and how great your power is to sustain it. Even harder to comprehend is the indisputable fact that you care for something so small as myself in this vast universe. Thank you for sustaining me. May I remember, when it feels I'm crashing and burning, it's you who is holding me together, keeping me in flight. Thank you. Amen.

Worship: "Center" by Charlie Hall, "Everything To You" by Bethel Music and "Color" by Upperroom

56

Sin's Deceit

But encourage one another daily, as long as it is called "Today," so that none of you may be hardened by sin's deceitfulness.

HEBREWS 3:13

We find sin's deceitfulness all over the marketplace of life's choices. Satan packages it beautifully. With glimmering charm, sin invites us to pleasure, self-satisfaction, and fulfillment. However, this is simply the surface value of sin in the market of life and the false advertisement Satan uses to convince us to buy.

Have you ever fallen for a product that promised to change your life but didn't? We see them on TV all the time—from glue that bonds large water-soaked objects together like new to a system for organizing pan lids that promises to change our lives. Like any false advertisement, sin makes promises, a step up in the game of life, but its warranty expires sooner than the small print indicates. There is no lifetime guarantee. The payoff for buying-in is fleeting. The master of false marketing, Satan, cannot deliver what he promised and, in fact, never intended to. It's a scam!

When one product fails, we look for the new and improved. The jolt of short-lived pleasure becomes an addiction and, like any other addiction, makes a mess of our lives. We thought the gossip would make us look like we're in-the-know, the affair would solve the deficit in our love life, or the lie would get us out of a bind. We soon find it is dynamite, set on a short timer, and wrapped up in a deceitfully pretty, little package—what the writer of Hebrews calls "sin's deceitfulness."

Sin's destruction goes beyond our own lives, straight to the heart of God himself. Our sin grieves the Lover and Redeemer of our souls (Psalm 78:40) and puts distance between us and him (Isaiah 59:2). Sin is addictive, habit-forming and soon begins to rule our lives. Though it starts out small, each little choice we make to sin further callouses our hearts until we stop trying to make better choices for ourselves, stop caring that others are hurt, and stop noticing the gap forming between us and the only one who can truly satisfy.

Sin is like the frog in the pot of boiling water. If a frog is placed directly into boiling water, it will jump out. But if the frog is put in water at a comfortable temperature and then brought to a boil slowly, it will not realize its danger and slowly die. We are much the same. When we're young and introduced to a violent, gory, or scary movie, we are initially shocked and disturbed. The more movies we watch of that nature, the less likely we will feel that unease designed to get our attention. Sin in our lives is much the same. We become tolerant of the evil within ourselves and in the world around us—what the writer of Hebrews calls "hardened." Though our sin seems insignificant at the time, a gentle step toward sin turns into entanglement in sin incognito, wreaking havoc on both our hearts and our ability to hear and trust God.

If only we could see our future selves after sin has had its way with us. If only we could see beyond its deception at first glimpse. If only the sober young man could see his future forty-year-old drunk self abusing his wife and kids, he may not have ever picked up a beer. If only the woman could see the pain in her best friend's eyes as their friendship dissolves over hurtful words spoken behind her back. She may have protected her best friend's reputation instead. If only the gambling man could see his future of more loss than gain, he may have chosen not to head to the casino and offer his life savings. If only the cheating man who gave in to the little affair at the office could see his wife, two weeks later, walking out the door with his kids and half the money, only to turn back and find his mistress no longer interested, he may have ignored the come-ons of his charming coworker.

Sin is deceptive and blinding, slowly boiling us to our death. Although we don't always realize there's a fire under our pot, sometimes others can see the flame and give us warning. When we have become calloused, how good it is to have true friends who are willing to reveal to us that pot is being heated. Let's jump out before it's too late!

Reflection: What beautiful package have you bought into only to find the promised pleasure was a lie? Is there an area of your life where you have been "hardened by sin's deceitfulness"? What sin previously bothered you, but no longer has that effect?

Prayer: God, it's hard to believe I could be in a pot, slowly coming to a boil without realizing. Forgive me for allowing my heart to harden and for buying into the deceptive little package of sin. Thank you for the insight of others. Help me to be open to receiving that truth and to take it with my defenses down. Rescue me from the pot I'm in. Amen.

Worship: "Slow Fade" by Casting Crowns and "Glorious Day" by Passion

57

Encourage One Another

But encourage one another daily, as long as it is called "Today," so that none of you may be hardened by sin's deceitfulness.

HEBREWS 3:13

Have you ever watched a friend make a choice you knew would bring about their own demise? It's like watching your close buddy walk toward the edge of a cliff. The friend doesn't see the drop, but you do, and you want to scream for them to stop, to warn them there's a drop ahead! In the world of physical danger, you would scream without hesitation, but in the world of emotional and spiritual cliffs, you may dissuade yourself. However, when a friend is walking toward his spiritual demise, it's no less vital.

The Greek word for *encourage* in this verse is *para-kaleo* and means to come alongside, to warn, to bring comfort, to instruct, or to strengthen. Having close relationships with other Christians means we watch one anothers' backs. Sometimes our own demise can be prevented by others who see clearly what we have become blind to in our sin. A true friend encourages us away from our cliffs at the end of a path enticed by deceitfully marketed sin.

It is our responsibility as fellow believers to encourage one another through prayer, love, compassion, and a commitment to love them no matter what. As the close friend of one in trouble, we must have the courage to speak to them with many considerations in mind. First, before any counsel is offered, we need to listen to gain understanding of the whole situation. Hear others out without judgement, always remembering the "plank in our own eye" (Matthew 7:3-5). Asking questions is good way to engage a friend without judgement and allow them to tell their own story. We must ensure love governs our words, expressions, and body language and that love is our strongest message. We must convey we are simply one beggar telling another beggar where to find bread—and we are in this *with* them. We are not self-righteous administrators of others' lives but equal partners on a journey together.

On the flip side, we all need to create space in our lives where permission is always granted to our close Christian friends to spur us on to righteousness. When we're approached with a matter of sin in our lives, we need not feel singled-out because everyone—even those we think are impenetrable—needs encouragement from time to time to resist temptation. Nor is there anyone too low in muck and sin who doesn't need encouragement to rise. Refusing the gentle guidance of someone who loves us is like saying, "No thanks, I'll just stroll off the cliff."

Like a pack of wolves preying on the stragglers falling behind the rest of the herd, so Satan goes after the Christian believer who isolates himself from the body of Christ. The command to come alongside another in Hebrews 3:13 can't be followed until we're approachable. It doesn't happen unless friendships are rich, deep, and transparent. Gathering on Sunday morning is important, but it, alone, is not enough to cultivate the type of friendships that spur us on toward godliness. This depth of relationship doesn't happen during the "turn and greet your neighbor" time slot or the small talk on the way out the door of the church. We must be intentional about pursuing these deeper relationships that lead to honesty and encouragement. Rich relationships require time—intentional time. We need to remain open to grow and mature. We need to create the space in our hearts for extraordinary brotherhood.

Reflection: Is there someone in your life walking toward a cliff, yet you have not had the courage to speak? In what ways have you noticed a friend, family member, or spouse encouraging you toward a good path? Have you been open to constructive criticism in the recent past? If not, why? How can you be intentional about pursuing deep friendships that are transparent and encourage you to grow?

Prayer: Lord, God, I wish I could see things clearly and get by on my own, but I know we were created for community. Help me to connect closely to others, enough for them to know my struggles, and for me to be able to offer kind encouragement to them as well. Soften my heart and help me to accept the words of my spouse and my friends when they encourage me toward the right path. I pray my words of encouragement toward others would be kind, gentle, and loving and I would be sensitive enough to approach them at the right time and with the right words. Amen.

Worship: "Brother" by NEEDTOBREATHE and "Who We Are" by Courtnie Ramirez

58

Unwholesome Hearts

Do not let any unwholesome talk come out of your mouths, but only what is helpful for building others up according to their needs, that it may benefit those who listen.

Ephesians 4:29

What is "unwholesome talk"? Some think "unwholesome talk" is certain four-letter words. However, when we take the whole verse in context, it implies unwholesome talk as words that are destructive to others. Refraining from saying @#$&, yet attacking another's character, is no better than the hearts of the Pharisees, following their man-made laws and completely missing the spirit behind the command.

Unwholesome talk and destructive words: I'm guilty of this. You're guilty of this. Every single one of us. We can be mean! We think mean things, judge those we believe are making poor choices, have impatience for people who disagree with us, and hold bitterness against those who've wrong us. The mean words we speak begin with our thoughts. Though we try to hold in these thoughts, they slip out of our mouths and spread dark clouds over those around us. Out they shoot—cruel and cutting words, orders barked at others, arguments, lies, put-downs, complaints, words that destroy others' reputations.

God knows the damaging words come from an impure spirit—a spirit not fully surrendered, not seeing others through his eyes—a desire for others to see us as better than them. If our minds and hearts are full of negativity, it will slip out and wound others. This is the reason God doesn't simply want us to bite our tongues, he wants sincere change in our hearts. When our hearts are surrendered, the wholesome talk follows.

We cannot change our hearts with our own strength. We can't simply make a decision to speak wholesomely from this day forward and BAM!—no more unwholesome talk. We need heart transformation only given through God. God assures us, "I will give you a new heart and put a new spirit in you; I will remove from you your heart of stone and give you a heart of flesh" (Ezekiel 36:26).

How do we get this "heart change" from God? Just as something that glows in the dark needs to be placed near a source of light to glow, so do our hearts. When we keep close to the Light, we can glow in a dark world so desperately needing light (2 Corinthians 4:6, Matthew 5:14-16). After spending time in God's presence, soaking in his powerful light, our glow will, by response, build others up.

Let's consider the effect we have on others. We have the power to make or break someone's day. When we take time to get our glow on, our relationships will have more harmony, life becomes more positive and peaceful, we find greater success at work, and we prevent a heap of trouble in our lives. I know there is so much work to be done and it is difficult to find the time, but we must be intentional about seeking God for a changed heart so we can get our glow on and light up the world!

Reflection: Of these areas, which do you struggle with the most—insensitivity, impatience, barking at others, lying, putting others down, yelling at family members, prioritizing being "right" over having harmonious relationships, holding grudges, or complaining? Are there areas of your life that are not fully surrendered to the life changing power of God? Which area will you surrender today?

Prayer: Lord, God, please get my attention before destructive words leave my mouth. Please give me a heart transformation. May the thoughts coming from my heart reflect gratitude and positivity. May I see the best in others, have compassion and sensitivity, and replace harmful words with life-giving, wholesome words. Help me find the time to get my glow on each day. Amen.

Worship: "Bullets" by NEEDTOBREATHE and "Changed" by Sanctus Real

59

The Life-Giving Power of Building Another Up

Do not let any unwholesome talk come out of your mouths, but only what is helpful for building others up according to their needs, that it may benefit those who listen.

EPHESIANS 4:29

The best exercise for our heart is lifting others up. Ironic how building up the hearts of others, in turn, elevates our own. Building others up is so important, Paul says we are to speak only when the purpose is to build others up—only if it will benefit them. Otherwise, we are not to speak!

What are some practical ways we can build up others?

- Encourage others. Many times, we notice something admirable in another, but we just keep it to ourselves. We need to make it a habit to let others know we notice the good in them.
- Choose to be kind, even when others have chosen otherwise.
- Offer grace. Although some people may deserve our piercing words, we are called to give undeserved favor—grace.
- Choose joy and spill it onto others who lack joy.
- Express gratitude rather than complaints.
- Ensure our words come across in a gentle and loving tone.

Words have the power to bless or to break another.

Children, especially, need our wholesome talk. When our children disappoint us, we sometimes let them get the best of us. We yell at them, scold them, or shame them because we expected so much more! These types of harsh reprimands could devastate their souls. While they do need correction, the lesson is better learned through consequences without the unwholesome, destructive words. Words easily wound a child's spirit, in some cases, for years to come. However, consequences given calmly cause them to think before acting the next time. It's the consequences that speak to their actions, and the destructive words that speak to their spirits. Children, more than anyone, need "helpful [words] for building [them] up according to their needs." They need us to catch them doing something right and give them frequent affirmation.

Husbands and wives have incredible power over their spouse's self-image, dignity, and sense of worth. Use that power delicately and wisely. Of course, you want your spouse to feel as if he or she has value, but it's hard for them to feel of any value when they are constantly being torn down by their other half. When having a disagreement, try a different strategy. Don't try to "win" the argument. Rather, try to "win" the prize of self-worth for your spouse and his or her trust in you. Think about the topics you argue over, how you argue about them, and how you can "win" together. Sometimes, it's through gentle confrontation, allowing them to see your side in a considerate way. Sometimes it's keeping your mouth shut and praying. Sometimes, it's giving up on your own selfish way and allowing another way, even if it isn't the "best" way.

Let's touch base on another part of this Scripture that often gets lost: We are to build another up "according to their needs." We are all different in the way we receive another's words. The way I would love to be encouraged may not go over as well by someone else. Something we might say with all good intentions might come across as hurtful to another person. Furthermore, we shouldn't pass off another's pain just because we can't relate. We must be sensitive enough to find out the needs of that individual along with their unique circumstance. By listening more and seeking to understand others, we can learn how to build others up "according to their needs." Do they need a strong intervention or a gentle word of concern? Do they need more listening and less preaching? Do they need words of understanding or words of correction? God knows the specific needs of others. So, first and foremost, it is imperative to seek God's direction in building others up "according to their needs."

Let's agree, no matter the circumstance, to speak words of life to others. Agree to spread love, joy, and peace through our words. Agree to spend time each day to get our glow on so we can build one another up according to their needs.

Reflection: In what ways do you need to get better at building others up? Did you relate with directing unwholesome words at your kids? Or winning the argument with your spouse? Have you taken the time to seek God's direction with your words to meet the needs of others? Do you tend to pass off others' pain when you can't relate? How can you show compassion to others who have different sensitivities than you? Make a mental note to be more intentional about letting others know when you notice something good in them.

Prayer: Lord, God, sometimes I'm more focused on the words I say than the spirit behind them. Help me to uplift others, no matter how angry they have made me, and no matter if it's deserved. I don't deserve your grace, yet you pour it on me without limit. I pray you would help me to be sensitive, even when I can't relate to the struggles of others. May my words build, rather than demolish, those around me. Amen.

Worship: "Words" by Hawk Nelson and "Your Words" by Third Day

60

Thoughts to Reality

Finally, brothers and sisters, whatever is true, whatever is noble, whatever is right, whatever is pure, whatever is lovely, whatever is admirable—if anything is excellent or praiseworthy—think about such things.

Philippians 4:8

Changing our quality of life is possible through changing our thoughts. This doesn't seem feasible, but it's scientifically proven. The *Law of Concentration* states whatever you consciously and persistently direct your thoughts upon will grow and expand into reality in your life. In other words, the more you think and reflect on something, the larger impact it will have on your daily choices, behavior, and actions. When we constantly dwell on negative thoughts, then negative conditions will increase in our lives. If we dwell on positive thoughts, then pleasant conditions will grow and increase in our lives. What we think about is what we look for, and we usually find what we're looking for.

The Bible addresses this concept in Proverbs 4:23. The NIV says, "Above all else, guard your heart, for everything you do flows from it." The Hebrew word for the *heart* that we are to guard is *leb,* which refers to the will of the inner man. *Leb* could also be translated to mean attention. The New Century Version translates this verse as, "Be careful what you think, because your thoughts run your life."

In some circumstances, we have choices to make. However, sometimes life drops us into situations with zero options. We didn't have a choice about which country or family we were born into. We couldn't choose the way were raised. We can't change the past. We have no control over the weather or the actions of others. Many things in life are beyond our realm of influence. However, we do have control over one thing and that is our thoughts which have more to do with our quality of life than we would imagine.

When we find ourselves up the creek without a paddle, our choices may be limited, but we can still choose our thoughts and beliefs. We can simply endure the difficulty, grit our teeth and bear it, or worse yet, wallow in it—or we can choose to look for, and enjoy, the good in the midst of it. We can grumble about our lemons or squeeze them into water, add some sugar and make the best we can out of them. We can see everything as a tragedy, or we can look for the way God reveals himself in the adversity. We can wallow in self-pity or rise to the challenge as a warrior ready to conquer the enemy. We can focus on the obstacles blocking our way or seek out new opportunities to challenge us and cause us to grow. We can focus on our inadequacy or God's great sufficiency. Choosing to search for the good in life will benefit not only ourselves, but those around us.

Are you ready to change your life trajectory? Begin with your thoughts.

Reflection: Do you tend to see situations with pessimism or optimism? Can you think of a situation that changed once you were able to see it in a new light? What difficult situation are you currently facing? How could you change the way you perceive it?

Prayer: Lord, God, I admit sometimes I feed the negativity in my mind and let it grow. Sometimes I don't see a way out of my troubles and, honestly, I'm not even looking for your hand in my hard situations. I pray you would bring awareness to my thoughts. Help me to see the good in everything, to knead in some fun wherever I can, and to change my perspective. I know you will bring me peace and joy with a renewed line of thinking. Thank you in advance for that. Amen.

Worship: "God Is Good" by Francesca Battistelli and "On My Way To You" by MercyMe

61

Training Our Thoughts

Finally, brothers and sisters, whatever is true, whatever is noble, whatever is right, whatever is pure, whatever is lovely, whatever is admirable—if anything is excellent or praiseworthy—think about such things.

PHILIPPIANS 4:8

Satan leads us to the pit of the earth and leaves us there. He wants us in a state of blindness to all things good, so he lies to make us believe the worst. He aspires to convince us we're in a dead-end place with no hope. One of his favorite avenues to keep us in the pit is whispering exaggerated, irrational thoughts. He loves it when we throw ourselves a pity party, blame others, and assume the role of the victim. He revels in our jealousy, anger, defensiveness, hatred, pride, and fear.

Common lies Satan whispers include: *No one likes you. You're at the bottom of the social ladder. You're an incompetent parent—just look at your kids' behavior. You are invisible. No one will ever love you. You are not as good [smart, pretty, competent…] as everyone else. You are a train wreck, a hot mess, damaged goods. You will never reach your goal. You'll never be promoted, never get out of debt, never repair that broken relationship, never overcome your addiction. This is the end of the road for ever finding happiness again.*

Do any sound familiar? Do you sometimes pay so much attention to the lies they eventually become your truth, despite *the* truth? Have you ever bitten into one of those lies and let it fester to the point you were debilitated, to the point you actually changed course of action because of that belief? If you have, Satan got you exactly where he aimed.

These lies are debilitating and flashed to us over and over again in neon lights. Do you know why? Because Satan is panic-stricken over the power we hold. He doesn't want us to realize who we are, and the stuff we're capable of, when God is on the throne of our hearts. The great truth is that *we* have the power, not Satan. Satan is the artist of deceit, but much to his dismay, he is not the commander of our minds. We are in control of what we allow to make a home in our minds. Oh, how he wants to have that power, but it's only ours!

For most of us, thoughts are unintentional, like a sailboat moving in the direction of the blowing wind. A thought comes out of the blue, a trail of thoughts follow, and the next thing we know, we've been blown into a certain direction unintentionally. However, we do have the ability to control the direction we move by training our thoughts. We are usually careful about how we spend our money, prioritizing what is most important to us. So why aren't we doing the same with our thoughts? If our thoughts control so much of the quality of our lives, why are we not careful where we allow them to go?

When Satan blows our sails with the whispers of his lies, we don't have to drift along in that direction. By choosing thoughts that are true, noble, right, pure, lovely, admirable, excellent, and praise-worthy, we resist going to the pit of the earth. Let's manage our thoughts wisely and sail on toward truth and excellence.

Reflection: Were any of the above-mentioned lies relatable? What other lies are you allowing to be blown into your sail? Take some time to consider your thoughts as a budget and re-prioritize your "spending." What's staying and what's going?

Prayer: Father of Truth, sometimes I buy into lies [list out which lies you tend to buy into]. Help me to recognize them as lies when they're whispered to me. Help me to take control over the direction my sailboat moves. May I only allow thoughts that are true, noble, right, pure, lovely, admirable, excellent, and praise-worthy. Please help me to stay in control of the direction I move. Amen.

Worship: "Fighting Words" by Ellie Holcomb and "Voice of Truth" by Casting Crowns

62

From Pit Dweller to World Changer

Finally, brothers and sisters, whatever is true, whatever is noble, whatever is right, whatever is pure, whatever is lovely, whatever is admirable—if anything is excellent or praiseworthy—think about such things.

PHILIPPIANS 4:8

Tragedies happen. Often, we find ourselves in places where we can't find anything worthy of praise—a child dies, a spouse cheats, a family member takes his life. All unspeakable atrocities. When facing heartbreak, we need to mourn and grieve our losses. We can face the sorrow knowing that "The LORD is near to the brokenhearted" (Psalm 34:18 NASB). Then there comes a time when we need to get back up and carry on. This can be so difficult. God is calling us, and enabling us, to look for the good that comes out of what seemed only loss, and to dwell on it, bask in it, and find healing in it. We must search for the positive, though it's challenging, and keep bringing our thoughts back to that—the lovely, admirable, excellent, and praiseworthy.

You may be thinking, *Sounds easy for some to say but they haven't been through what I'm going through. They don't understand.* Surprisingly, the author of this verse, Paul, went through insanely horrendous situations. You may be surprised to learn that Paul, before having a life-changing encounter with Jesus, had killed many people. He had the blood of innocent people—Christians specifically—on his hands. After his conversion, he was used by God to grow the Christian church exponentially. Paul was never far from the memories of his past as he mentions them often in his writings. If he had let his thoughts linger on his past, if he had dwelt on the fact that he killed so many people in pursuit of stopping church growth, he could not have moved as far and fast as he did. He could have allowed his guilt to debilitate him. Instead, he set his mind on the positive.

Is it any wonder Paul became a world-changer? He well understood the power our thoughts have over us. When a negative, condemning thought came to his mind, I imagine he said, "Not today, Satan!" then continued on his way, spreading the gospel. We can't let our thoughts cripple us. Let's think with intention and allow our focus to stay on that which we want to enlarge. Get out of that pit and go!

Reflection: Give each quality in this verse some thought. Who do you know that is noble? Who do you know that is right-standing? Who do you know that is pure? Lovely? Admirable? Excellent? Praiseworthy? Who do you know that could easily allow their thoughts to debilitate them but chooses to move forward instead? How can you remind yourself to replace negative thoughts with positive truths? Sticky notes? A daily journal where you list something in your life that relates to each quality every day? Daily prayers of gratitude?

Prayer: Dear Lord, thank you for giving me your Spirit who empowers me to have control over my thoughts and allows me to move in a positive direction. Fix my heart and mind on you and on these positive qualities. Help me to recognize unhealthy thoughts and replace them with healthy, positive truths. I pray I will not live in a debilitated state. Please use me to be a world changer. Amen.

Worship: "Rise" by Danny Gokey and "I Choose To Worship" by Rend Collective

63

Yoked With Christ

Come to me, all you who are weary and burdened, and I will give you rest. Take my yoke upon you, and learn from me, for I am gentle and humble in heart, and you will find rest for your souls. For my yoke is easy, and my burden is light.

Matthew 11:28-30

In the time this was written, farmers used yokes on their oxen—a kind of collar with a wooden beam placed between to keep the animals together. The yoke was then attached to another object, such as a plow, so the animals could pull it with combined strength. To train young oxen, farmers partnered them with stronger and more experienced oxen. The job of the younger ox was simply to follow in the same direction and keep the same pace as the older, more mature ox. As long as the young ox followed the older ox, the work was easy and brought fruitful, productive results. If the younger ox decided to rush through the task, veer in another direction, dawdle, or refuse to move, the work became much more difficult. Only when the younger ox walked in step with the older ox could the younger ox do what was required of him without collapsing from exhaustion.

Oxen were not the only ones using a yoke in those days. People, individually, also wore yokes across their shoulders as a frame intended to balance loads at each end. Heavier loads require less energy when balanced and evenly distributed. These were familiar images to the people when Jesus taught that only by taking his easier, lighter yoke, and learning from him would we find rest for our weary souls.

Our idea of a lightened load is for God to remove our difficulties *completely* and tell us to run and be free! Sound about right? We think we simply need to ask God to remove our problems and make our lives easier while we go on our merry way, unchanged. However, God has a different plan in mind. He doesn't always remove our burdens but gives us another yoke instead—a different, lighter, balanced yoke. This yoke is tied to him. He wants to lighten our load, but to do so, we are required to walk in-step with him. This means we are communicating with him, getting to know him, and learning to understand him and his ways that are higher and greater than our ways. We are asking him for direction, trusting him, and believing his promises because he is faithful. He *wants* to carry this load with us. What an excellent accommodation—a bargain we can't turn down!

Reflection: What heavy load have you been carrying lately? When you feel Jesus's leading, nudging you to go a certain way that is against your own will, do you fight, or do you follow? Are you in step with Jesus? What actions can you take to lighten that load and walk-in-step with him?

Prayer: Lord, Jesus, thank you that I don't have to carry my burdens alone. I forget that I am not required to carry it alone. I am grateful you so strongly desire relationship with me and to teach me new ways. Thank you for proving yourself over and over so I can fully depend on you without fear. Help me to surrender to your ways which are so different from my own. Amen.

Worship: "Rest For Your Soul" by Austin French and "We Dance" by Bethel Music

The Yoke of the Law

Come to me, all you who are weary and burdened, and I will give you rest. Take my yoke upon you, and learn from me, for I am gentle and humble in heart, and you will find rest for your souls. For my yoke is easy, and my burden is light.

MATTHEW 11:28-30

In the teaching in Matthew 11, Jesus refers to the "yoke of the law." God had set a standard, given through Moses, for his people to live by—a set of rules to follow, in essence. These laws were impossible for people to follow, proving no matter how hard we try, we are incapable of reaching God's level of holiness. The law was not intended to give life (Galatians 3:21). To the contrary, the law was considered a "ministry that brought death" (2 Corinthians 3:7), and offered no wiggle room with God, no hope.

If the law wasn't difficult enough, along came the Pharisees, a legalistic group, who complicated the law even further, adding even more regulations to expound on each law. For example, the law required them to do no work on the Sabbath. The intention of this law was to give them a day to rest. It makes sense then that they would not sow an entire field on that day. The Pharisees decided if one walked through a field and unintentionally rubbed against a plant, knocking seed to the ground, he was guilty of "sowing" and therefore of breaking the law to rest on the Sabbath. The legalistic Pharisees became more concerned about keeping the law for the sake of appearances while their hearts rotted inside.

The Law of Moses, in itself, was not criticized. In fact, many Jews found solace in the law. David described his love for the law and the security and solace it brought him, multiple times (Psalm 1:2, Psalm 19:7-9, Psalm 119). Jesus wasn't criticizing the law, only the self-righteous misuse of the law common among the Pharisees. Through Jesus's perfect life of obedience (the fulfillment of the law), he took the burden of that law from us. Jesus wants for us, when we come to the end of ourselves (even better, *before* we come to the end of ourselves), to surrender to his grace and accept his gift of righteousness.

Though we cannot keep this impossible law with perfection, we are covered by the grace offered to us through Jesus. It is only through faith in him—not works, not anything we can *do*—that we earn righteousness. We simply need to believe and trust God (Romans 4). The yoke of a life lived by faith is easier than the yoke of impossible works. He wants for us to take his yoke of righteousness and to rest in his grace.

Reflection: Take some time to think about the yoke designed for us to carry, the law. Then think about the yoke offered to you through Jesus.

Prayer: Jesus, thank you for removing the yoke of futile striving to obtain a righteousness I cannot reach. Thank you for giving me a lighter, easier yoke of faith to bring me to the Father. You say to come to you, that you want me to learn a new way from you. Please teach me your ways so I will find rest for my soul. Amen.

Worship: "Real Love" by Blanca, "Satisfy" by WorshipMob, and "Covered" by Planetshakers

Yokes We Carry in Vain

Come to me, all you who are weary and burdened, and I will give you rest. Take my yoke upon you, and learn from me, for I am gentle and humble in heart, and you will find rest for your souls. For my yoke is easy, and my burden is light.

MATTHEW 11:28-30

Our human nature tends to take on more than our souls can carry. As we learned in the prior devotion, the Pharisees struggled with the yoke of the law, earning salvation through works—perfect works to be precise. Before we go judging them for carrying a load that was never intended for them, let's check ourselves. Are we carrying loads we were never intended to carry alone? Are we like the prideful Pharisees, carrying loads to impress those around us? Are we carrying a burden by ourselves to prove self-sufficiency—even though God sent someone to help, did we turn them away? Are we saying we are saved by grace, not by works, yet still feel we aren't doing enough to earn salvation?

Other unnecessary yokes we carry could be anxiety, self-reliance, pride, striving to keep up with the Jones's, anger, frustration over things out of our control, fear, busyness, hopelessness, guilt, low self-worth, and self-pity. Maybe we spread unnecessary drama, prove our worth through achievements, or crave constant entertainment. All of these are burdens we were never intended to carry, weighing down our yokes.

Jesus's yoke is peace, joy, unconditional love, forgiveness, patience, hope, faith, trust, humility, gentleness, self-control, and surrender. It is releasing grudges and loving others well. It is embracing peace when the world tells us to be anxious. It is biting our tongues before releasing hurtful words that will never be unheard. It is choosing to see through an optimistic lens of hope and joy. It is a clear understanding of our worth that comes from who we are in him.

When we are weary, we tend to first look to other people or things to bring us comfort. We tend to only go to God as a last resort. But Jesus is saying he wants us to approach him first as he is the only route to true rest for our souls. We have nothing to lose, except our exhaustion, and everything to gain!

Reflection: In which of these areas do you find your load is heaviest: anxiety, pride, perfectionism, trying to keep up with the Jones's, anger, frustration over things out of your control, fear, busyness, craving constant entertainment, hopelessness, creating unnecessary drama, proving your worth through achievements, guilt, low self-worth, self-pity, victimhood, or self-sufficiency? Which of these qualities of Jesus do you need increased in your life today: the ability to comprehend your worth in him, the ability to love others well, peace, joy, the courage to forgive, patience, hope, faith, trust, humility, gentleness, self-control, or surrender?

Prayer: God, thank you for offering me an easier yoke when I walk in step with you. Thank you for promising me rest for my weary soul. Help me, when I'm tempted to carry my own load, to instead apply the life-giving, restful yoke you offer. Amen.

Worship: "Broken Ladders" by Selah and "Let It Go (Everything)" by Deitrick Haddon

66

Contentment

Keep your lives free from the love of money and be content with what you have, because God has said, "Never will I leave you; never will I forsake you."

HEBREWS 13:5

Does this make anyone else stop and ask *What do these two things have to do with each other—freedom from the love of money and God's promise to not leave or forsake us?*

It seems God is trying to tell us the love of money is dangerous. What is the "love of money"? And why is it dangerous? Who doesn't love money? Am I sinning because I love money?

The "love of money" has more to do with our hearts and less to do with what we have. It's not wrong to enjoy what money can buy. Sometimes, God decides to bless us with abundant wealth—take Job for example. Physical blessings aren't wrong. What is wrong, even dangerous, is when we crave the satisfaction it brings, when we depend on it to satisfy our hearts. It's to our detriment to believe the notion it will give us a sense of security, a sense of power, more options, or lavish experiences. Desiring more and more is a trap that keeps us imprisoned. We need to work longer hours, get that promotion, change careers. We're always chasing more and more money and more and more stuff. As soon as we get what we want, we're on to the next thing we must have to bring us contentment. We want more than our own hands can hold.

However, things disappoint. How many times have we bought something we wanted—clothes or a new "toy"—and soon found we didn't care for it anymore? Or invested a lot of money into a new hobby that soon disinterested us? Everything we own—yes, everything—will one day be in a dump. There are no exceptions. That gives a whole new perspective on things. When will we learn that nothing satisfies us for long?

What if we could have all those things—power, more options, lavish experiences—with a deeper relationship with God? It's possible, but not on our terms. The options, the experiences, the power, the security may not be the same as what we had in mind. It's a different kind of power, different options than we thought possible, and a different kind of experience, but richer and more satisfying for the soul. Furthermore, we don't have to change careers or work longer hours to get it.

There is a God-shaped hole inside each of us. Though we try to stuff things in there to fill it, they're the wrong shape. We will never be satisfied until we fill it with the precise thing that fits. Why did God even design that hole in us? Could it be that his desire to fill that space is just as strong, or stronger, than our desire to have it filled? He created us with longing for him and he is passionately pursuing each of us. He longs for each one of us to allow him to quench our desires. Since he also created that hole in each of us, he alone knows exactly how to fill it, for it is the shape of him.

There is our answer. The reason those two things—freedom from the love of money and God's promise to never leave us—are put together in one verse. The love of money is the wrong shape. Our true contentment comes from God. He is with us, and that is enough. When we truly find contentment in him alone, we can come to a state of mind where we can say to God, *You can take away anything I have and I will be as content as I was before. I never really owned any of it anyway. It was always yours. You are enough for me.* That's the proof of authenticity. Can we say with Paul, "I have learned to be content whatever the circumstances. I know what it is to be in need, and I know what it is to have plenty. I have learned the secret of being content in any and every situation, whether well fed or hungry, whether living in plenty or in want"? (Philippians 4:11-12). That's deep down, soul-satisfying, rest-giving, heart-mending, peace-giving satisfaction. That is the place God wants us, the place he can use us the most. That is the place we will be most deeply satisfied in our innermost being.

Reflection: What have you been dreaming of that you would really like to have? What would your life look like if that possibility were taken away from you? Would you be content? What do you own that, if taken from you, would bring you deep grief? Do you find it hard to trust God to bring you contentment? What steps can you take to fill all your desires with God alone?

Prayer: God, thank you for all the good things you have given me [list them out]. I know that you are the one who provided all those things. Help me to hold my belongings loosely. I trust you with all of it. God, please reveal areas of my life that are leaving me feeling unsatisfied. Fill me with so much contentment in you that I don't crave anything else. Amen.

Worship: "Provider" by Cade Thompson and "After You" by Britt Nicole

67

Working Heartily

Whatever you do, do your work heartily, as for the Lord and not for people, knowing that it is from the Lord that you will receive the reward of the inheritance. It is the Lord Christ whom you serve.

COLOSSIANS 3:23-24 NASB

Sometimes we do a shoddy job with half-hearted effort, especially when we feel others, such as our boss or those we live with, don't deserve our wholehearted commitment to the task. This verse commands us to work "heartily as for the Lord"—not for people—and was written to the people in Colossae, many of whom were slaves. How hard it must have been for a slave stripped of freedom, dignity, and privileges, to work heartily for his master as if he was laboring for God himself. We are called to the same high standard.

Paul instructs us to work "heartily." The word *heartily* concerns the attitude. It's an attitude of passion, exuberance, and sincerity. Imagine two carpenters hired to build a wood deck. Who better reflects Christ? Carpenter Tim, wearing a shirt proclaiming, "In God We Trust," whose finished product looks as if it could fall over with the next breeze or Carpenter Todd who crafted a sturdy deck with additional structural reinforcements, just for good measure, while wearing a t-shirt promoting his favorite rock band? The quality of the work we do reflects the difference God has made in our lives.

The reason we are commissioned to work "as for the Lord," is not because he is dependent on us to do certain jobs. It's not about us meeting God's needs. It is about God meeting our needs. It's not uncommon for people to go to other countries for "missions work" to help the people there but return home having been richly blessed and radically changed by the people whom they went to serve. It's like that. When we work heartily as if for the Lord, God's blessing outweighs the work.

We may have no choice about our responsibilities on the job, our work environment, or whom we work with, but we do have a choice whether we make it a pleasant experience for ourselves and the people around us. If we want to make it a positive experience, here are practical ways we can change our attitudes from resentful to hearty:

- Don't complain.
- Choose joy and laugh often.
- Be open to feedback.
- *Ask* for feedback.
- Don't cut corners.
- Choose kindness.
- Encourage others.
- Go the extra mile—even for people who don't deserve it.

Reflection: What jobs bring out the worst in you? What jobs do you dread? What does it mean to you to work heartily as if for the Lord in your home, workplace, or place you volunteer? Have you ever been blessed more by those whom you intended to bless? Which of the above listed ways to change your attitude can you incorporate into your life?

Prayer: Thank you, God, that even though I don't always enjoy the work I have to do, I *have* work and purpose. Please remind me that you require hearty effort, good quality, passion, and sincerity in all I do. I pray the attitude of my work is an accurate reflection of all you have done in my life. Amen.

Worship: "Fade With Our Voices" by Jason Gray, "Live Like That" by Sidewalk Prophets, and "Work" by Tedashii

68

As You Wish

Whatever you do, do your work heartily, as for the Lord and not for people, knowing that it is from the Lord that you will receive the reward of the inheritance. It is the Lord Christ whom you serve.

COLOSSIANS 3:23-24 NASB

Does your attitude on the job and quality of your work vary depending on the amount you're paid? If you're paid thirty dollars an hour to mow Mr. Smith's lawn, you'll probably do a better job and pay better attention to details than you would with Mr. Anderson's lawn job that pays ten dollars an hour. Oftentimes, the quality of our work depends on how well we're being paid. Good news! God is generous and his pay scale is beyond our wildest dreams! Sometimes he provides us with earthly treasures. But *all the time,* he is depositing our pay into "an account" awaiting us in Heaven (Matthew 16:27). The reward God gives is more valuable than any paycheck, promotion, or accolades we'll receive here on earth and, best of all, it's insured and cannot be taken away. Sometimes we feel we're working hard for pennies while others who work minimum-effort jobs get the big bucks. Parenting is one of the most difficult duties on earth and pays absolutely nothing monetarily. But remember, though we may not be receiving a handsome pay for our work here, God is paying well, and he is asking us to do the job with *his* rate of pay in our hearts and on our minds. He calls for our best ability—not cutting corners, not complaining—but, working with absolute sincerity and devotion to the task. When we notice our attitudes taking a downward shift, let's take a deep breath, and remember we're working for the best boss ever.

In addition to working heartily for the Lord, Christ expects us to lower ourselves to the position of a servant to others. Though Jesus was called the King of the Jews, he willingly took on the role of a slave when he washed the feet of his disciples. Washing feet was not an uncommon task in those days. In our time and culture, washing our neighbor's feet when they stop by would pose an awkward situation. But in that part of the world, the sand and wind mixed with a pair of sandals made for some dirty feet and it was common for guests to get their feet washed upon entering a home. That job was delegated to the slaves. It was a job others felt "above" doing. When Jesus washed the feet of the disciples, it was a radical statement, *Do what others feel they are too over-qualified, or too distinguished, to do and do it with sincerity.* There is no job too lowly, no person too great.

I think of the movie *The Princess Bride.* From the very beginning of the movie, the farm boy, Westley, so in love, utters to Princess Buttercup whenever she asks him to do something (which she does often), "As you wish..." He was so in love with her, he would do anything for her, humbly and gratefully. It was through his actions and servant-like spirit he expressed his love for her. And so it should be for us, whenever we are tasked with anything. Loving God and committing our lives to him means our response to his request to serve others heartily should be, "As You wish..."

Reflection: If you began doing all tasks "as for the Lord" rather than your employer, fellow volunteers, or family, what would you be doing differently? Are there any jobs you've felt should be left for others in a "lower position"? Consider doing these jobs with a humble and grateful attitude.

Prayer: Father, forgive me for the times I have thought I am better than others and have left some tasks to others that I could have done myself. Thank you, Jesus, for your attitude, humbly serving and showing us no one is too high and mighty. Thank you for paying well with rewards that await me. Help me to remember that next time I'm grumbling about my wages. May my work be for you—a reflection of the lowly servant you became. I look forward to the day you return and say, "Well done, good and faithful servant." Amen.

Worship: "Do Everything" by Steven Curtis Chapman and "Take My Life" by Chris Tomlin

69

Eager to Listen

My dear brothers, take note of this: Everyone should be quick to listen, slow to speak and slow to become angry.

James 1:19

Due to living in this fast-paced culture with modern technology, we are used to getting what we want instantly. We don't like to wait. Forcing ourselves to slow down, to quiet our minds, and to be present in the moment requires effort. And effort is exactly what is required of us to listen when someone is speaking. Listening is a skill and, just as in any other skill, we must put in the effort to cultivate it.

This Scripture says to be "quick to listen." The word *quick* conveys a spirit of eagerness, readiness, and willingness. Remember when we were in school and the boring teacher sounded like the teacher on Charlie Brown, "Wa wap wa wap wa..."? Then, we heard her say, "This will be on the test." Suddenly we tuned in, eager to hear what we needed to know! This is the kind of eagerness we should have when others are speaking to us.

All too often when others are speaking, we are not really listening, rather we are planning what we will say next. Then we interrupt to interject our thoughts before the conversation shifts. Without realizing, we are viewing our thoughts as more important than another's. Philippians 2:3 calls us to view others as more important than ourselves. One way we can do this is through intentional listening, without interjecting our own thoughts. This means we are storing away what we have to say for the moment and absorbing what the other person is telling us. When we view others as more important than ourselves, it follows that we will have genuine interest in what they say.

Listening requires not just putting a plug in our mouths, but intentionally hearing what the other is saying. It is not thinking about the next thing you're going to say, or about the frozen meat you forgot to pull out of the freezer to thaw, or the fact that you once again forgot to call your child's doctor. Intentional listening is a mindful practice—pushing everything out of the mind to deliberately focus on others. Having 3 jobs and 4 kids, I can sympathize. Having a busy lifestyle and a lot on the mind makes listening very difficult.

If you, like myself, are not a very attentive listener, here are some active listening techniques you could try.

- Ask active listening questions like, "What I'm hearing is..." and "Sounds like you are saying..." The occasional question or comment lets others know you're listening and helps you stay tuned in to them. In addition, it clarifies what they mean and prevents misunderstanding.

- Don't prepare a rebuttal while the other person is talking. Listen for the purpose of understanding, not for the purpose of interjecting your own experience. Remember that it's not necessary to "top" others' stories with a better one of your own.

- Listen for the purpose of supporting others, not to find fault in them, correct them, or criticize them.

- They may not be asking for your opinion. It might be that they only need to sort their feelings out loud, they want someone to understand where they are coming from, or they just want to be heard. It could be that they would like advice, but we must first determine if they are asking for the advice before we give it. Unwelcome advice comes across as judgmental. To be sure they want advice, ask, "Do you want my opinion and advice? Or do you just need to vent?"

- Don't interrupt. Interrupting another mid-sentence says you are done with what they have to say and are ready to enlighten them with your own thoughts. Interrupting is the opposite of being quick to listen.

The second part of this verse states we are to be "slow to speak." Do you know someone who talks way too much? When you picture this "talker," do you think of them as a wise person? Likely not, as it is impossible to gain insight when doing all the talking.

Not by chance do we stumble upon wisdom. It is only gained through the effort of listening or reading. Some of us talk so much we miss the insightful gems of others' experiential wisdom. Let's not miss one opportunity to gain wisdom because we are busy with incessant chattering.

Reflection: Recall the last conversation you had. Did you do more of the talking or more of the listening? Which of the above active listening skills could you put effort into further developing?

Prayer: God, reveal to me whether I do more talking or listening. I pray you give me the ability to focus on others, undistracted, without feeling the need to interject my own thoughts. May I value others above myself and impress upon them that I care and appreciate their words. Amen.

Worship: "Self Less" by Josh Wilson and "Lay It Down" by Matt Maher

70

Slow to Anger

My dear brothers, take note of this: Everyone should be quick to listen, slow to speak and slow to become angry.

James 1:19

In our society, we overload our schedules. We have a plethora of things to get done and an overabundance of concerns on our minds, causing us to become tightly wound. Then the little things, which normally don't bother us, prompt us to snap! My husband and I have been experiencing a stressful situation for several years. I didn't realize, until Joel pointed it out to me, that I had started snapping very quickly and easily over trivial things, whereas I hadn't snapped that easily in the past. I had allowed myself to become wound too tightly. If it's possible, we need to lighten our loads before we reach that breaking point.

"Snapping"—or losing control—is thought by some to be normal as if it's not possible to control the volcano inside. You can't always control the way things make you feel, but you do have complete control over your reactions. Have you ever been so angry, you "blew up" at someone, then your phone rang, and you suddenly gained control of your anger, set it aside, and answered your phone with a polite greeting? This is because we do have control of ourselves.

When we let our anger get in the way, rationality goes out the window. We are no longer thinking clearly and logically. Groucho Marx said, "If you speak when angry, you'll make the best speech you'll ever regret."[8] I have found, I have far more influence with others when I have a cool head and speak gently. When I'm not in *attack-mode*, others aren't in *defense-mode* and are more willing to listen.

Let's apply James's advice to social media as well. Social media can get us so riled up. It's too easy to post a snappy reply, a harsh comment, or a huffy, snide remark. We can delete our harsh comments from social media, but not from someone's heart. It's a good idea to make it a practice never to post when angry. That might mean in a few minutes, but it could also mean a few days. If it really needs a reply, it can wait until we've had time to cool down. Once we've prayed about it, God may tell us to let it go. Sometimes, our best move is to remain silent, focus on the condition of our own hearts and allow God to speak to the one who offended us. If their heart is open, he will speak to them at the right time and in the perfect way. If their heart isn't open, why do we think *we* could reach them?

Reflection: Is there something you need to release from your busy schedule so you're not so tightly wound? What circumstances cause you to "blow"? What can you do to gain control over your anger before lashing out? How can you become more aware of your tone and the way you are coming across to others?

Prayer: God of Peace, show me where my schedule may need adjusted to allow myself occasional times of serenity. I pray I can remain calm and peaceful when stressful events come my way. Please give me control over my anger. Remind me to stop before I say something, or post something, out of anger. Help me to let go of the need to set people straight when they frustrate and anger me. Amen.

Worship: "Heartbeat" by Aaron Shust and "Peace" by Jadon Lavik

71

God's Delight

He brought me out into a spacious place;
he rescued me because he delighted in me.

2 Samuel 22:20 (also Psalm 18:19)

A child takes delight in an ice cream cone loaded with sprinkles. Teenagers are delighted when sharing times of laughter with their best friends. Spouses delight in the romantic gestures shown to them. And God delights in you. Delight occurs when we enjoy an experience or the companionship of another. Does it boggle your mind that God delights in you?

Maybe you've been treated by others as an inconvenience. Maybe people have stepped on you to get to the top. Maybe you were the object of another's own personal bitterness. Maybe you were let down by someone you trusted. Being knocked down in life by others has caused you to struggle with feeling that someone, especially a God who seems so far away, could ever delight in you.

The Bible tells us a few of God's sources of delight. We know God delights in his Son (Isaiah 42:1, Matthew 3:17), the nation of Israel (Ezekiel 16:8-14), and you (Zephaniah 3:17). Yes, *you* are on the list with Jesus! Have you been bullied by the world? Are you overweight? Are you wrinkly? Do you walk with a limp? Are you socially awkward? Were you overlooked when the party invitations went out? Do you feel the world is less-than-delighted with you? Guess what: God, the one who really matters, delights in you! He enjoys you. He takes pleasure in you. You're his "ice cream cone with sprinkles."

No need to waste your energy earning the delight of people who don't matter. You are already enjoyed by the One who matters most. God created you with your unique quirkiness, your odd sense of humor, and atypical personality. You don't fit the norm because God wanted variety. He wanted you.

Why did God want you? God didn't create you because he wanted someone to annoy him. He created you because he knew you would bring him delight. He enjoys and desires your companionship.

We are often annoyed by interruptions and needy people, but Jesus didn't show annoyance when the crowds of people followed him, interrupted him, and imposed themselves on him with their needs. No, that's us people who feel that way about others. What annoyed, and even angered, Jesus were those who felt they didn't need him. But he delighted in those who sought him. He loved those whom the world rejected. It's easy to be confused when the world has made you feel unlovable. Be careful not to mix up what the world has done to you with the God who delights in you. People have limits. We have deadlines for productivity, limited energy, and sometimes apathy. Many people have little time, energy, and patience for interruptions by others. God has all the time in the world, unlimited strength, and infinite energy. He isn't pestered by your search of him, your need for his help, or by your relationship with him.

If there is no back-and-forth camaraderie, no intimacy, or no fellowship between you and God, it wasn't God who left the relationship. So come to him with boldness, with all your quirks and anomalies. He is there, waiting for you with all the time and energy in the world, because he delights in you.

Reflection: What delights you: eating a particular food, creating art, reading, fishing, dancing, a sport…? What do you feel when you're doing this activity? Whose company do you most enjoy? How do you feel when you are with this person? Take a moment to reflect on how God has those same feelings toward you.

Prayer: Creator, God, thank you that you are not a Father who simply tolerates me. Thank you for loving me, even delighting in me. It feels good to know you enjoy me. Knowing you delight in me brings healing to my broken places. When people turn their backs on me, remind me you have never turned away. Forgive me as I have turned away from you at times. I pray for deeper fellowship and intimacy with you. Amen.

Worship: "Even At My Worst" by Blanca and "I Am Loved" by Maverick City Music

72

Mutual Delight

He brought me out into a spacious place; he rescued me because he delighted in me.

2 Samuel 22:20 (also Psalm 18:19)

Now that we know God delights in us, how are we going to respond? It's good to bask in the knowledge that God delights in us. It's like water to our parched souls. However, what are our reasons for absorbing his delight? Are we using this information simply to boost our self-importance? Or are we using this information to reciprocate our delight back to him, hone our focus on him, and build intimacy in our relationship with him? The Word tells us to delight ourselves in the Lord (Psalm 37:4). It's a two-way street.

The account of Mary and Martha reveals to us that relationship with Christ is more valuable than anything we can *do* for him (Luke 10:38-42). Mutual delight between God and people—being delighted in and, in return, delighting in him—is the secret to rest for our souls. When we "get" this, our focus is removed from our productivity or abilities.

When we get it, we will rest. When we get it, our negative self-talk will vanish. When we get it, worldly success no longer defines us. When we get it, we will be satisfied because God's delight is all we ever needed. When we get it, our faith in God's delight sustains everything we do. Yes, we go through valleys just like every other person, but through the struggles of life, we lean in closer to God. God's delight colors our perspective of every situation, counterbalancing the difficult times with God's love and strength.

Reciprocating God's delight starts with our thought life. Satan loves for us to forget God's goodness and to become distracted from who we are—God's delight. Delighting in God means identifying Satan's lies and replacing them with God's truth. For example, when our thoughts turn to self-defeat, *You're not good enough*, we trade that thought in for *God's grace is enough and even more powerful in my weakness* (2 Corinthians 12:9-10). Or when we think *No one wants me*, we trash that thought and bring to mind, *God chose me and loves me dearly* (Colossians 3:12). When we feel despair, *My life is miserable and won't get any better,* we instead choose to focus on the hope God promises, *God has great plans for me to thrive and will come to my rescue* (Jeremiah 29:11, 2 Timothy 4:18).

When you're feeling discouraged, search for Scripture pertaining to your current struggle, for example, "Scripture for hopelessness" and meditate on those verses. You'll find, the more you do this, the more free and rested you'll feel.

Another way we reciprocate delight in God is to allow nature to enlighten us. God reveals himself through his creation (Psalm 19:1-2, Romans 1:20). I am convinced a beautiful sunset is God wooing me into courtship with him. Lightning teaches me his power is unmatched. A forceful waterfall reminds me God is strong enough to carry me through my trials. A peaceful brook reminds me he quiets my soul. The birds remind me not to worry because God provides (Matthew 6:25-34). The intricacies of a delicate flower remind me he cares about the details of my life.

There are parts of God we miss when we are separated from nature. I encourage those living in urban areas to be intentional about spending time in nature, delighting in God's handiwork. Consider the reason why God places such beauty on the earth. It isn't for himself—he has all the beauty of Heaven. It is a gift for us to enjoy. He doesn't have to give us a brilliant pink, orange, and purple sky. He does it to delight us.

Gratitude is another practical way to delight in God. Count your blessings. Express thankfulness to God for them, write them in a gratitude journal, meditate on them and share them with others. Gratitude fuels delight!

God expresses his delight in us through singing (Zephaniah 3:17). And we can, in response, delight in him through singing as well. The Bible has over four-hundred references to singing. Fifty times we are commanded to sing. The longest book of the Bible, Psalms, is a collection of songs for God. It seems singing is important to God! There must be a reason God doesn't simply ask us to *say* praises to him. He wants us to *sing* them! When we sing, the words penetrate deeper into our minds. Not only that, songs speak to our emotions, moving the truth from our heads to our hearts. The passion in the music dissolves our apathy. When we sing about God's provision and sovereignty, worries fade away. When we sing about God's goodness, our hope is restored. Grieving our sin puts us in our rightful, humble place. Giving God praise for our personal victories puts credit where it's due. Celebrating God's grace gives us lasting joy.

The Psalms are full of songs about *every* emotion we feel. David sang about God's provision, and we saw his worries fade away in song. He sang about God's goodness, and his hope was restored. This may be another reason David was called a man after God's own heart. How better to delight in God than to have our hearts beating in rhythm with him through song.

Delighting in God gives meaning to life. Bask in God's delight. Respond with delight in him. Keep in step as reciprocated delight becomes a harmonious dance.

Reflection: Are there ways not mentioned here that you delight in God? What lies tend to pop into your head? What truth can you replace it with? Write that truth down and place it where you'll be reminded. What are you grateful for? What emotions do you feel when you sing to God? Consider taking a trip into nature and asking God to reveal himself to you, then watch for it.

Prayer: God, lover of my soul, thank you for creating me with intentions for me and you to delight in one another. I pray I would notice when you are revealing your love to me and I, in turn, would be captivated. Teach me to delight in you as well. Amen.

Worship: "Indescribable" by Beckah Shae and "The More I Seek You" by Gateway Worship

73

God's Pursuit Through Adversity

"For I know the plans I have for you," declares the L*ORD*, *"plans to prosper you and not to harm you, plans to give you hope and a future."*

JEREMIAH 29:11

Jeremiah 29:11 has been an encouragement to Christians and Jews for centuries. Many of us have it memorized. It's a declaration we lean on, a promise we take comfort in. Who doesn't want to prosper? However, in our pursuit of prosperity, we often take this verse completely out of context. We see it standing alone on a graduation card, a mug, a t-shirt, a plaque on the wall, or a piece of jewelry but never does that card or plaque go into the surrounding verses. If so, it might say, "You're going to live in difficult times for seventy years, so settle in and remember I have plans to eventually pull you out of the suffering."

God's people, the kingdom of Judah, were being punished. They had fallen into the very wicked, Godless culture of the surrounding nations. They had inconceivably sacrificed their own children in the fire to another god. God had sent prophets to warn them of their sin and the consequences of it, but they killed those prophets. So, in 597 BC, God demanded their attention with not-so-subtle means. Nebuchadnezzar attacked Jerusalem, taking 10,000 captives back to Babylon. These people of Judah lost everything. False prophets were trying to offer encouragement, telling them God would soon rescue them as he had in the past. However, Jeremiah, God's authentic prophet, told them this was not truth and God was not about to rescue them. (Their rescue didn't come for another seventy years!) God's plan was not to pull them out of their suffering, but to teach them something through it and to draw them closer to him.

One would think after falling into such outrageous sin of sacrificing their own children and killing prophets, God would say, "Forget it! My people have fallen too far and are undeserving of rescue!" However, as is his nature, his love does not quit. He was not done pursuing them and is not done pursing us! His love is fierce, and he chases after us in hot pursuit. God uses all means possible, including the storms in our lives, to spur us to seek him, to grow and mature into the rich, spiritual prosperity he has planned for us. His game plan is not for the storm to destroy us, but that we would learn to thrive with him in the midst of it.

Mistakenly, when we read this verse standing alone, we think God is promising us a tranquil cruise to health and wealth and all things we consider perfectly wonderful. But the surrounding verses here speak of suffering in exile. It's not that God enjoys watching us suffer. It's that he has a higher plan than we can see with our limited point of view. His ultimate plan for us, as seen in the surrounding verses, is for us to have relationship with him, no matter the circumstance. He will allow whatever situations and use whatever means possible to accomplish that goal. If we learn to hold tight to God's ways and our relationship with him, in the end we prosper.

Reflection: What trial are you going through currently? Is it possible God has caused or allowed this situation as a means of grabbing your attention? In what practical ways can you choose growth in your "captivity"?

Prayer: Dear God, thank you for pursuing me despite the times I've turned my back on you. I know it is not always your plan to pull me out of my storm, but to draw me close to you. I pray you give me strength to get through this storm. Help me to use this storm as an opportunity to seek you, to draw closer to you, and to grow stronger in my faith according to your plans for me. Amen.

Worship: "Nothing Between" by Sanctus Real and "The Valley Song (Sing Of Your Mercy)" by Jars of Clay

74

Standing on the Promises of a Hope & a Future

"For I know the plans I have for you," declares the LORD, "plans to prosper you and not to harm you, plans to give you hope and a future."

JEREMIAH 29:11

As we learned in the previous devotion, it was while held in captivity in Babylon, the people of Judah sorted out their faith. It just might be through our own painful situation God is prompting us to sort out our faith as well. Disappointments, trials, pain, and loss are inescapable. However, we have a choice. We can become discouraged or even angry with God, turn away and choose spiritual death, or we can stand on the promise and accept the "hope and future" planned by God, specifically for each of us.

Standing on the promises of "a hope and a future" seems like the right choice. So, how do we choose to do that? It's not the easiest route but it's the most rewarding. We lay down our idea of what prosperity looks like and the dream we conjured up of what our lives should be. We choose obedience over comfort, sacrifice over greed, faith over doubt, perseverance over mediocrity. When we take this difficult route through God's boot camp, that's when we find genuine prosperity. In a sense, it's like we're working through grueling university grad courses while holding on to the hope of graduating into prosperity.

Rob Kenney, referred to as the "internet dad," was abandoned by his father at the age of fourteen, and so moved in with his newlywed brother. He later married and hit a bumpy road. While expecting a baby, Rob lost his job, and it felt to him like everything was falling apart. Through his struggle, Rob cried out to God to get him out of his mess. It was then he began reading the Bible and seeking God. God had plans for Rob's future. Having a heart for those struggling with a broken family or absent parent, Rob created a successful YouTube channel called *Dad, How Do I?* Here he reaches thousands of young people with "practical 'Dadvice' for everyday tasks." His videos cover topics such as how to tie a tie, how to change the oil in the car, and inspirational poetry with an "I'm so proud of you" message for his young listeners so desperately in need of encouragement. I imagine Rob came to a point in his life where he lifted his pain up to God and said, "What am I supposed to do with this?" And God told him exactly what to do with it.

When we go through a storm that rips our hearts to shreds, if we seek God in prayer, if we dive in to learn his heart and ways, if we choose to worship him—even through our pain—God will guide us to his plan to prosper us and he will give us a hope and a future.

Bring your pain to the Throne and ask, "God, what am I supposed to do with this?" I guarantee the answer won't be to wallow in it or to whine about it. You may be blown away by what God wants you to do with it.

Just a few verses earlier, in Jeremiah 29:7, God says, "Also, seek the peace and prosperity of the city to which I have carried you into exile. Pray to the Lord for it, because if it prospers, you too will prosper." God told Judah to seek good for the nation who held them in captivity—their enemies! He called them explicitly to pray peace and prosperity over them, for as their captors prospered, so Judah would prosper. His people were to settle into their circumstances. They were to live among their captors in peace. In like manner, when are circumstances aren't about to improve, we are called to settle into our circumstances, to seek God in our adversities, to live in peace and to pray for those who oppose us in life. His plan is to prosper us where we are. As we surrender to that plan and trust him with our future, hope abounds.

Reflection: Bring your pain to the Throne and ask God what he wants you to do with it. How can you choose to trust the promise of "a hope and a future" in your specific situation? Do you desire for those around you—those in authority over you, those who have harmed you, or those with whom you subconsciously compete—to prosper as well? How can God use you to bless those around you?

Prayer: God, I had such a pretty picture of what my life would look like but I'm far from it. Help me to lay down my dream of what prosperity looks like, to not hold so tightly to my pretty plan. I want to seek and worship you even though I'm in pain. Help me to find the time to dive into your Word without distraction, to learn your heart and your ways, and to choose sacrifice over comfort. Help me to be a support to others in their storm and to bless the world around me. Amen.

Worship: "Rise Up" by Matt Maher and "Hope And A Future" by Housefires

75

Complaining

Do everything without complaining or arguing.

Philippians 2:14

We are born crying. It is not until six weeks later we show our first sign of delight—a smile! Complaining is deeply engrained in our human nature. It peaks during the "terrible twos." *Even though I threw a tantrum yesterday because I wanted applesauce, Mom should know that doesn't mean I like it today!* We eventually learn to control our outrage over these seemingly unjust situations. At about age four, most of us are beginning to learn some social norms. We notice other humans aren't throwing themselves to the ground in an award-winning display of drama because Mom said "no" to a donut for dinner. It's an uphill climb from there for us all. Even at age sixty-five, we're still squawking about trivial matters. Since grumbling is deep-seated within us, it takes conscious effort to overcome.

One would think people living on "Easy Street" would be joyful while those with bleak circumstances would be the grumbly ones. However, Americans are some of the most pampered people on earth, and surprisingly, the biggest whiners. We are entitled. We believe we deserve better and are worthy of so much more—and how dare others not "recognize"! On the other hand, in *all* the third-world countries I've visited, I came to know some of the happiest, most grateful people. It doesn't seem circumstances affect our attitudes as we would expect.

Also, in America, political grumbling has reached its peak, and not just among politicians. Somehow, we think our arguing and grumbling is going to change minds and fix the world, but it only creates a deeper divide. Fierce conversation over the state of our world reveals hearts that don't trust God holds it all in his hands, don't believe God sets up kings and takes them down (Daniel

2:21), or that God is as active in government today as he was in Moses's day when Pharaoh was at his mercy. It is possible to stay informed and involved politically while also putting our trust in God, even when things turn in the opposite direction than we think best.

Another popular arena for grumbling and arguing is social media. That is a swamp of negativity and endless complaining. I challenge you to a social media self-examination. To gain a perspective of your own attitude, look at the last twenty posts you have made. If most of your posts were negative, you may have a bigger problem with grumbling than you realized. If this is you, try withholding from the divisive conversations altogether and train yourself to do more listening. When you do speak (post or comment), do it with understanding, respect, and humility.

Complaining is a sin, detestable to God (1 Corinthians 10:10, Numbers 11:1, James 5:9). It's one of the sins we often overlook. Most of the time, we don't even consider it a sin because we're all so prone to it. We think we're each entitled to a "grumpy day" or we "need to vent." There is a difference between a spirit of complaining and seeking advice through hard times. Talking to someone about what we're going through and listening for another's advice is healthy. In fact, within a marriage, communication about *all* details, the good, the bad, and the ugly, is vital to a healthy relationship. While it is out of line to tell all who will listen for the sake of stirring them up against our offender, stating the problem to a trusted friend or family member in search of a solution is not in the spirit of complaining.

Our relationships will suffer when we choose a lifestyle of grumbling. Nothing is attractive about spending time with someone who finds fault with everything as "Negative Nancy" drains the life out of us. We know we've become a problem when others, after spending time with us, need to go recharge alone.

Not only does grumbling affect those around us, but it also has a monumental effect on the way we experience life. Maybe that's why God significantly despises complaining. It depletes the abundant life he wants to give us.

Though we can't avoid disappointments, we can choose to what extent they will affect our lives. Is the problem all we can see? Or are we searching with hope for a way out? Are we pulling up a recliner, kicking up our feet, and settling into that dark pit of disgruntlement? Or are we refusing to dwell there and choosing gratitude instead?

To fight our chagrined spirits, first we need to become aware when we are complaining, then be intentional about changing gears. Bite back the complaints and, instead, seek God's hand in it, look for the positives in the situation, and offer the benefit of the doubt. Discuss solutions to the problems instead of spouting out unending negativity and self-pity. Take the grievances to God in prayer, leave them at the Throne, and venture back into life with a renewed spirit. Gratitude enriches our quality of life and transforms what we have into "enough."

Reflection: Take some time right now to look at your past twenty posts. Do you tend to spout negativity or spread encouragement? What are you most prone to complain about? What positive things can you see in the circumstances you complain about? What effect has your grumbling had on the people who must listen to it? Do others need to go recharge alone after spending time with you? How can you hold yourself in check to change your thoughts?

Prayer: Father, I'm sorry when I forget complaining is something you detest. I get comfortable with griping. I forget you require better from me. The next time a complaint comes to my mind, help me to remember you can make beauty from ashes and to search for that in expectation. Give me solutions and opportunities to rise above the things I complain about. I will be on the lookout for ways out of my problems even if it requires thinking outside the box. Amen.

Worship: "Smile" by Sidewalk Prophets and "These Days" by Mandisa

76

Gratitude—The Light That Shines

Do everything without complaining or arguing.
Philippians 2:14

When I worked in a hospital, during *hospital week,* my employer would provide a lunch for their hundreds of employees to express their gratitude for our hard work. I was happy to not have to pack a lunch or buy food that week! However, I was soon brought down by some coworkers who were griping because they work so hard and all they got for *hospital week* was a lunch. My cheerful mood was quickly brought down by the grumbling around me.

Complaining is contagious. Like a toxic disease, it works its way into our souls. It's too easy to join in with others kicking up a fuss. Not so easy to do the opposite and swim upstream. If our coworkers complain, our spouse complains, our friends complain, and we are reading a barrage of complaints on social media, we're bound to catch the disease. But here's the bright side—all emotions are contagious. Enthusiasm too! If our emotions are going to transmit to others, what would we like others to catch?

Complaining literally affects brain and body function. A 2016 study by Stanford researchers found that complaining shrinks the hippocampus, which is the part of the brain critical to problem solving. This means our griping is limiting our ability to think a way out of our problems. In addition, complaining releases cortisol, the stress hormone, which raises the blood pressure and blood sugar. Frequent complaining can also lead to heart disease and diabetes. Those are some heavy consequences for our bad attitudes, something completely under our control.

So how can we stop grumbling and complaining? We can't simply take something away without replacing it. Gratitude is the perfect substitute. There is also scientific research regarding gratitude and its effect on our brains and physiology. According to a multitude of studies, gratitude enhances empathy, reduces aggression, brings about better sleep, improves self-esteem, increases mental strength, increases dopamine, lowers anxiety and depression, boosts the immune system, and makes us more productive. Whew! That's a whole lot of benefits!

We tell our kids all the time it's okay to be different—and we absolutely mean it! We know in our hearts that *different* is just what the world needs. Likewise, our Father calls you and me to be different. He says to let our lights shine in the darkness (Matthew 5:16). We live in a dark world that craves illumination. What better way to be a light in darkness than to live in gratitude, share good news, and look for God's hand of provision. Disgruntled people are not world-changers. So, let your light shine so brightly that others can find their way out of the dark.

Reflection: What current situation has you grumbling? Is there something good in this situation you can turn your focus toward? What emotions are you transmitting to others lately? How can you foster a spirit of gratitude?

Prayer: God, forgive me when I choose grumbling over gratitude. Help me to let my light shine in the darkness and spread positivity everywhere I go, especially in my own home. I want to turn my home in to a place my family *wants* to be—a place of healing, a place to grow, a place of respite from the hard knocks of life. I need your strength to transform me. Amen.

Worship: "Thank God For Something" by Hawk Nelson and "Let There Be Light" by Josh Wilson

77

Love That Abounds

And it is my prayer that your love may abound more and more, with knowledge and all discernment

Philippians 1:9 ESV

Love that "abounds" was high on the list of things Paul prayed for (1 Thessalonians 3:12, 2 Thessalonians 1:3). But what *is* love that "abounds"? I'll tell you what abounding love means to me. There are times I reach the end of my rope and I don't think I have one more ounce of love to offer. Then, God steps in to provide me a little bit more love to give. There are times I conjure up in my head all the things I want to say to someone and I'm ready to go "tell them off." But before I open my mouth, the Holy Spirit intervenes and softens my words with compassion and gentleness. There are times my children push my buttons until I reach my boiling point but instead of lashing out at them, I suddenly get a grip on my control and speak calmly. Sometimes I think I don't have it in me to serve the ungrateful, high-maintenance person one more time, but then I'm reminded and given strength to go one more mile (Matthew 5:40-41). There are times I decide there's no way I can let go of a personal injustice one more time, but I am surprised by the strength I have to forgive, yet again, one more time. It's at these times I think I used my last drop of love, but I'm astonished to find there is love beyond myself, a "rainy-day fund" of God-empowered love, renewing my heart. That, to me, is love that abounds. It springs from a never-ending supply.

Abounding love is not something we can accomplish on our own but is the result of God pouring into our hearts as we continue to say *yes* to our highest calling, love. When our love abounds more and more, it is like a natural spring which never runs dry, a constant current flowing outward keeping no water to itself but sharing and spreading outward. That is what God has called us to and empowered us for. Abounding love, given abundantly and freely. If we miss this, we've missed our highest calling.

Reflection: Think of a time you reached the end of your rope with no more love to give, yet unexpectedly found the strength to keep offering love. Under what circumstances do you find yourself "at the end of your rope"? In what area of life do you need a little more love to give?

Prayer: Father, Supplier of never-ending love, thank you for giving your love so abundantly and freely. I have a finite limit of love to give, so thank you for offering your boundless supply every time I need it. May I tap into that "rainy-day fund" of love when my love reaches emergency lows so I can keep on loving the way you have in mind for me to love. Amen.

Worship: "Where You Begin" by Mandisa and "Letting Go" by Steffany Gretzinger

78

Loving With Discernment

And it is my prayer that your love may abound more and more, with knowledge and all discernment

PHILIPPIANS 1:9 ESV

That warm, fuzzy feeling of love. We've seen it in movies and read about it in romance novels. We've heard about it from a friend with the "perfect" marriage. It's there in our imaginations—gushy love that paints the world rosy red. Our culture tends to believe love is governed by the heart, not the mind. But love, according to God's Word, is not to be separated from "knowledge and discernment." Love, the command used here, is not blind affection, but instead, actions based on wisdom that comes from Jesus (v. 11). Love acts in unison with the mind.

Fulfilling the second greatest commandment in all Scripture—to love one another (the first command is to love God which is expanded as loving others)—requires knowledge and discernment so our love is expressed through words, deeds and actions that truly benefit the recipient. To love well is to love with sensitivity and insight into the other's heart. We are to love appropriately. This involves perceiving needs and recognizing how another individual receives love. It requires loving in ways that feel good and in ways that don't—both "warm and fuzzy" love and "tough" love.

Loving with discernment requires intention to perceive the struggles of others. We can't love and meet needs if we don't notice others. It takes noticing the quiet person at the party who would love to join the conversation but doesn't know the inside jokes. It takes recognizing that social cues and norms don't come easily to some who are trying to fit in but have a social cripple. It takes awareness of the person in the next pew struggling through worship, desperately in need of prayer. It takes realizing your spouse's emotional or sexual needs haven't been met in a while. It takes involving ourselves enough in others' lives that we recognize their needs so that we can meet their needs (love with discernment).

Love does what is best for the person being loved, not necessarily what makes the giver feel good. We tend to love others the way we like to receive love, but love must be tailored toward others as we're all so unique in the way we understand love. Everyone is different. Some people, during hard times, respond well to a little humor or a good time to distract them from their troubles while others might take offense to a playful jest during such perilous times and would rather have a sensitive ear and a shoulder to cry on. Some need space and alone time to process their heartache while others only spiral downward when alone and are best comforted in the presence of friends and family. Some might welcome and appreciate advice while others feel judged and disrespected by the advice of others. God-given discernment guides us into the best way to support others. To love with discernment is to see past the surface, find out the needs of others, and learn what makes them feel loved. Then love them uniquely.

Discernment prevents us from doing only what feels good in the moment. Sometimes love requires doing hard things—"tough love." Sometimes love is a boundary to prevent harm. Other times it's giving beyond the discomfort of the sacrifice. Sometimes it's a kick in the pants to help others achieve personal responsibility. Sometimes it's offering a meal or a roof. Love may mean discipline, or it may mean encouragement.

Love that is knowledgeable and discerning is fluid, taking on many shapes, and tailored to the needs of others. Let's let love flow adaptably, as God directs, to cover others.

Reflection: Have you ever been required to give tough love, an act of the will independent from feelings? Have you ever had to learn to love another in ways foreign to the way you typically understand love? In what circumstances have you shown love though it opposed your heart? How do the people in your life best understand or receive love differently than you? What steps can you take to learn their unique ways of receiving love?

Prayer: Wise and all-seeing God, thank you for your promise to give wisdom to all who ask. I pray that I would have awareness of those around me, that I would perceive when they have a need. Please give me wisdom and discernment to determine how to love them uniquely and effectively. Help me to draw closer to you so that love abounds more and more, springing up from that boundless supply. Show me ways to love others more and more and, in doing so, honor you. Amen.

Worship: "Jesus To The World" by NewSong and "Follow You" by Leeland

79

Excellence, Sincerity & Fruits of Righteousness

that you may approve the things that are excellent, that you may be sincere and without offense till the day of Christ, being filled with the fruits of righteousness which are by Jesus Christ, to the glory and praise of God.

Philippians 1:10-11 NKJV

Approving excellence, sincerity, filled with fruit… These verses have many treasures to uncover. Let's break it down piece by piece:

- "…that you may approve the things that are excellent…" What are the things that are "excellent" that we may approve? The J. B. Phillips translation uses the words *highest* and *best.* The world we see with our eyes vastly differs from the unseen, yet certainly existing, spiritual world. We see the earth, not the heavens. We see material plainly, but see only the effects of the spiritual. We are bound by time and decay while we await the unseen, indestructible life. While immersed in the daily battles of the visible world, it is difficult to remember the spiritual and eternal. Things that seem excellent to our carnal selves, may indeed be way off the mark by God's standards. That is the reason we need to be transformed, our minds constantly renewed, as we receive direction from the Spirit of God to know what is excellent, or "highest and best."
- "…that you may be sincere and without offense till the day of Christ…" This can be a confusing statement. Did Paul switch gears

mid-sentence to the subject of sin and the end times? How does this fit? Taken in context, Paul is making a powerful point. He's saying those who grow in love will become morally pure. The word *sincere* in Greek, *eilikrineis*, is two words compounded: *eili*, which refers to the splendor of the sun, and *krineis*, I judge. Put together, it means that which is judged in sunshine. If the brightest light were to shine into our lives, would it find any blemish hiding in the far recesses of our hearts? Would it find a selfish motive? If we're truly granting love that "abounds more and more" as discerned by our minds, we won't have selfishness cowering in the corners of our hearts. If we're completely sincere in our love, we won't need to panic when our hearts are laid bare in the light.

- "...being filled with the fruits of righteousness which are by Jesus Christ, to the glory and praise of God." This is the best part! The fruit of our labor! We cannot make fruit grow. We can prepare the soil, plant the seeds, water, and ensure it has exposure to sunlight, but we can't will it to grow. By the same token, we can't will ourselves to grow the fruits of God's Spirit: love, joy, peace, patience, kindness, goodness, faithfulness, gentleness, and self-control. None of these will be ours without love as Paul indicates here. The "fruits of righteousness" are a product of our growing love for and submission to God. They are assured when we draw near to him, nurture the conditions of our hearts, consume the daily bread of his Word, and expose ourselves to the light of his presence. Because God is love, when we do these things, we will produce fruit and love others well.

Choosing the highest and best, having purity in heart unadulterated by selfish motives, and producing fruit—these are the things that bring glory and praise to God.

Reflection: What varies significantly when seen through the lens of the tangible world versus the lens of the spiritual world? If a bright light were to shine into the hidden recesses of your heart, what would it find? Though you can't produce "fruit" on your own, what steps can you take to cultivate better conditions for the fruit to grow?

Prayer: Lord, God, as I'm limited in my view of situations, help me to have eyes for the excellent, the highest, and the best. I pray for purity, so when your light shines in the recesses of my heart, I would have nothing to hide. Help me to abound in love that grows "fruits of righteousness," used to love others and for your glory. Amen.

Worship: "Restore Me" by Kutless and "Hidden Places" by Vertical Worship

80

Above & Beyond Champions

No, in all these things we are more than conquerors through him who loved us.

Romans 8:37

Have you ever felt like life has brought you to your knees in utter defeat? Do you ever feel like you wake up each morning fighting the same demons you fell asleep fighting the night before and you're just too sapped to do it all over again? Have you ever felt like you're doing the best you can and the next thing you know, you've been ambushed by a series of unfortunate events? Have you ever felt like the paths you've chosen ended you in checkmate? That is exactly Satan's plan! He is not haphazard in his schemes against us. Rather, he prowls around like a roaring lion looking for someone to devour (1 Peter 5:8). A great tool of his: the feeling of defeat!

Satan wants to kill, steal, and destroy what God wants us to have (John 10:10). His plan is for us to believe we are small and weak, to feel overwhelmed by our troubles and so hopelessly confused about who we are and what we are fighting for. Why? Because the day we grasp the truth about who we really are and what we really can accomplish "through him who loved us," Satan is defeated!

Paul says we are "more than conquerors," translated from the Greek word *hupernikos,* a compound of *huper* and *nikos. Huper* means above and beyond, superior, or unrivaled. *Nikos* means overcomer, champion, or victor. Therefore, he is saying we are not only the victors, but we go *above and beyond* that status; we are unrivaled! Satan trembles at the thought of this.

Romans 8:37 starts with, "No." What is Paul saying "no" to? Just prior, in verse 35, Paul asks what can separate us from the love of God. Then he throws out some examples of what we might think could separate us from God's love—trouble, hardship, persecution, famine, nakedness, danger, or sword. The simple answer to all the above is "no." None of these things can separate us from his love. Paul is not referring to our love toward God. Neither is he referring to our *sense* of God's love toward us. God's love for us is an indisputable fact. It means no matter how we are feeling, we can't use our circumstances as a tool to measure God's love toward us. So, when we're feeling defeated, we must return to the facts and abandon the feelings. How we feel doesn't change the fact of God's love.

When we fully take hold of the unchanging, immovable love of God and the fact that our trials are not indicators of the amount of love the Father has toward us, our minds will be transformed. We will become more than conquerors. Knowing God's love is relentless—that nothing we encounter in life will ever separate us from him—gives us a new perspective. Suddenly, it doesn't matter how we feel or what anyone else thinks. God is *for* us, and we can rest in the knowledge he's got a plan to get us through what seems to us impossible.

Since we are above and beyond champions, let's make up our minds to live like we're the victors! Let's shed the loser-mentality, refuse the endless self-talk of defeat, and find our worth in the unchanging love of God. Regardless of past experiences, regardless of what someone once said we were, let's instead have confidence in the fact that we are more than conquerors.

Reflection: Do you tend to gauge God's love for you based on how good or bad your current circumstances? Do you live like the loser or the champion? In what ways would your life change if you remembered you are not the victim of your circumstances but the champion over them?

Prayer: Father, thank you for empowering me through your Spirit to live in victory. I don't want to believe the lies of Satan that I am defeated. You don't see me that way! Help me to see in myself what you see in me. Show me how to embrace the Warrior inside. Teach me to live in triumph. Amen.

Worship: "Victory" by Tye Tribbett and G.A. and "Conqueror" by Mali Music

81

On the Winning Team

No, in all these things we are more than conquerors through him who loved us.

Romans 8:37

"For your sake we face death all day long; we are considered as sheep to be slaughtered" (Romans 8:36). Romans 8:37 assures us we're conquerors, but just one verse prior, we are compared to sheep on their way to the slaughterhouse. It sure doesn't seem like "sheep to be slaughtered" are in a position to be "more than conquerors." Was Paul off his rocker? Or was he given a glimpse of us through God's eyes?

On our own, we are weak and vulnerable. Fortunately, we are not on our own! We are empowered by the one who cured the incurable, the one who commanded nature and it obeyed, the one who conquered the grave. Yes, *that* one is in us, empowering us to be more than champions! He wins the victory *for* us when we let him have the battle. The victory belongs to Jesus and all who claim him!

We are more than conquerors in *all* things. Victory over failures, victory over fear, victory over fatigue, victory over our broken hearts, victory over sin, victory over despair, victory over our circumstances. When we live in the truth that we are more than conquerors, everything changes. When we live in triumph, the devil is defeated and that sound of defeat can be heard by our families, our friends, and the world.

In Revelation, we are given a sneak peek of the final war where we emerge the final victors. We're on that winning team! No matter how wrecked our lives or how bleak the future looks, this promise gives us renewed strength to keep fighting through our current trials. Since we know the war is won, let's walk around in defeat no longer! Let's live as the conquerors God intends.

At the end of a battle, a soldier of the "winning" side goes home the victor and yet he does not feel joy in the victory. He may have been wounded. He may have lost a best friend on the battlefield. He may carry physical and emotional battle scars the rest of his life. In the wars of men on earth, there are sorrows, griefs, and losses that come along with the win. That is not the outcome of this spiritual battle in which we are soldiers. In our spiritual fight, the damages, the losses, and the scars of battle are worked out toward our own benefit and are in themselves, very much a part of the victory (Romans 8:28).

It's in our battles, we grow. It's in our failures, we develop determination and perseverance, bringing with it our victory. It's in our weaknesses, we see God moving more clearly because he is strong when our strength is depleted. In our grief, we gain wisdom and learn to rely on the Source that gets us through and will never abandon us in the battle. The things that initially look like defeat are the stuff of victory. When we believe this promise, we aren't devastated by the wrench thrown in our plans or the calamity charging our way. We know we are the victors, and we are ready for the fight!

Reflection: Reflect on battles you've faced in the past. What were their outcomes? Were you able to face them with full knowledge of and belief in this promise? What wounds resulted from the battle? How have these wounds been a part of the victory? What battles are you currently facing? How would your life change if you lived in the promise that you, through the Spirit of God, are an unrivaled match against evil?

Prayer: God, I thank you for inviting me onto the winning side. I know on my own, I'm simply a sheep on my way to the slaughterhouse, but you turn me into more than a conqueror. Help me to remember, when I'm experiencing what seem like losses on the battlefield, that you turn them into victory! I pray I would live in this promise. Amen.

Worship: "Be Fierce" by Here Be Lions, "Champion" by Bethel Music, and "Winning Side" by Israel Houghton

82

Getting What You Ask For

You desire but do not have, so you kill. You covet but you cannot get what you want, so you quarrel and fight. You do not have because you do not ask God. When you ask, you do not receive, because you ask with wrong motives, that you may spend what you get on your pleasures.

James 4:2-3

"You do not have because you do not ask God." WOW—that's great news! We want; we ask! But how many times have we, for our own benefit, taken this out of context? Sometimes we take this to mean we can have whatever we want, if only we ask for it. If we read further, we learn there are conditions of the heart that are prerequisites for receiving what we ask for.

You might appreciate the way *The Message* puts this verse: "You wouldn't think of just asking God for it, would you? And why not? Because you know you'd be asking for what you have no right to. You're spoiled children, each wanting your own way." We've got a double problem. First, we are by nature selfish and second, we don't see the big picture. Combine the two and BAM! That's why we "do not have." We want what we want without awareness of the grand scheme, and we want it with concern only for ourselves. Instead of trusting God to work things out for our good, we try to control God, reducing the Almighty Creator of the universe to a vending machine. We pop in the dollar prayer, push the button of our desire, and wait for the ordered blessing to drop down. When the blessing doesn't drop down, we pound our fists and curse the illusory vending machine.

"When you ask, you do not receive, because you ask with wrong motives, that you may spend what you get on your pleasures." What are we pursuing? Is it the will of God? Or is it our own personal desire for our own personal pleasures?

Our desire for self-serving pleasures begins to erode our prayer lives. We do not get what we want because we are asking, "My pleasures be bestowed upon me," rather than, "Your will be done."

God *wants* to give us wonderful gifts (Psalm 31:19). When we align our prayers with what God truly intended for us, he gives us what we ask. However, when we don't receive what we ask for, it's because his desires for our lives are different than our desires. Sometimes it feels like God has it out for us when a barrage of tragic situations crashes down on us, one after the other. The truth is, he does have our best interest in mind, and he wants us to trust that truth. But to receive from the Lord, we must give up authority over what is best and give God free reign. When we submit and obey, we realize what we thought we wanted has no value in comparison to the true gift God wants to give when we surrender.

When we come to know him better, we come to know what to ask for. God hears and answers prayers that are pure, based on his promises and free of our selfish desires. When we ask according to his will, which we can know by reading his Word, we will receive his perfect gifts in his perfect timing, not ours. An example was set for us by Jesus. The night before his horrifically pain-filled crucifixion, Jesus prayed in that darkest time for the hardest thing, "yet, not what I want, but what you want" (Mark 14:36 GNT).

Reflection: What is the "silliest" thing you've ever prayed for? What was your motive? Did you receive it? If so, did it fulfill you? Think of a time God gave you what you *needed* instead of what you *asked* for. What have you recently been setting your heart on? Are your motives for this longing self-serving or Kingdom-serving?

Prayer: Giver of every perfect gift, thank you that the desire of your heart is good for me. Sometimes I want things that serve me only, not realizing what's best. I don't mean to be so selfish but self-preservation and self-pleasure pop into my mind often. I don't have the whole picture, a strong love for all people, everyone's best interest in mind, and pure-as-white motives. God, I desire to be like you. Help me to keep my mind focused on your will in all things. I pray my desires would be for the right things with pure, unselfish motives. Amen.

Worship: "This Is Everything" by Audio Adrenaline, "Refine Me" by Jennifer Knapp, and "What You Want" by Tenth Avenue North

83

Promissory Notes to Take to the Bank

You desire but do not have, so you kill. You covet but you cannot get what you want, so you quarrel and fight. You do not have because you do not ask God. When you ask, you do not receive, because you ask with wrong motives, that you may spend what you get on your pleasures.

James 4:2-3

Can we pray for a new car? Can we ask God to help us climb the corporate ladder? Can we ask for our favorite sport's team to win? Sure! We can pray for whatever we want, but if it's not promised to us, we can't take it to the bank. There are many promises we *can* bank on. Basing our prayers on these Scriptures, we can have confidence we will receive what we ask for when his timing is right. Here is a list of promises we can pray with confidence that we'll receive:

God Will Fight For Us. "The Lord will fight for you; you need only to be still" (Exodus 14:14).

Strength. "He gives strength to the weary and increases the power of the weak" (Isaiah 40:29).

Renewed Strength. "…but those who hope in the Lord will renew their strength. They will soar on wings like eagles; they will run and not grow weary, they will walk and not be faint" (Isaiah 40:31).

Help & Support. "So do not fear, for I am with you; do not be dismayed, for I am your God. I will strengthen you and help you; I will uphold you with my righteous right hand" (Isaiah 41:10).

Wisdom. "If any of you lacks wisdom, you should ask God, who gives generously to all without finding fault, and it will be given to you" (James 1:5).

Forgiveness. "If we confess our sins, he is faithful and just and will forgive us our sins and to purify us from all unrighteousness" (1 John 1:9).

God's Presence. "The LORD himself goes before you and will be with you; he will never leave you nor forsake you. Do not be afraid; do not be discouraged" (Deuteronomy 31:8).

Provision of Needs. "And my God will meet all your needs according to the riches of his glory in Christ Jesus" (Philippians 4:19).

Comfort. "Even though I walk through the darkest valley, I will fear no evil, for you are with me; your rod and your staff, they comfort me" (Psalm 23:4).

Forgiveness & Love. "You, Lord, are forgiving and good, abounding in love to all who call to you" (Psalm 86:5).

Freedom From Fear. "The LORD is my light and my salvation—whom shall I fear? The LORD is the stronghold of my life—of whom shall I be afraid?" (Psalm 27:1).

To Walk in the Light. "I am the light of the world. Whoever follows me will never walk in darkness, but will have the light of life" (John 8:12).

A Full Life. "The thief comes only to steal and kill and destroy; I have come that they may have life, and have it to the full" (John 10:10).

A Fruitful Life. "I am the vine; you are the branches. If you remain in me and I in you, you will bear much fruit; apart from me you can do nothing" (John 15:5).

Honorable Qualities. "But the fruit of the Spirit is love, joy, peace, forebearance, kindness, goodness, faithfulness, gentleness and self-control. Against such things there is no law" (Galatians 5:22-23).

Peace. "Peace I leave with you; my peace I give you. I do not give to you as the world gives. Do not let your hearts be troubled and do not be afraid" (John 14:27), and "You will keep in perfect peace those whose minds are steadfast, because they trust in you" (Isaiah 26:3).

Reward for Kindness to Enemies. "If your enemy is hungry, give him food to eat; if he is thirsty, give him water to drink. In doing this, you will heap burning coals on his head, and the LORD will reward you" (Proverbs 25:21-22).

Direction. "Trust in the LORD with all your heart and lean not on your own understanding; in all your ways submit to him, and he will make your paths straight" (Proverbs 3:5-6).

Adoption Into God's Family. "Yet to all who did receive him, to those who believed in his name, he gave the right to become children of God" (John 1:12).

To Overcome the World. "For everyone born of God overcomes the world. This is the victory that has overcome the world, even our faith" (1 John 5:4).

Freedom From Sin. "For sin shall no longer be your master, because you are not under the law, but under grace" (Romans 6:14).

Power Over the Enemy. "Submit yourselves, then, to God. Resist the devil, and he will flee from you" (James 4:7).

Power, Ability to Love, Self-Control. "For the Spirit God gave us does not make us timid, but gives us power, love and self-discipline" (2 Timothy 1:7).

A Transformed Life. "Therefore, if anyone is in Christ, the new creation has come: The old has gone, the new is here!" (2 Corinthians 5:17).

Joy. "Those who sow with tears will reap with songs of joy. Those who go out weeping, carrying seed to sow, will return with songs of joy, carrying sheaves with them" (Psalm 126:5-6).

Healing From Brokenness. "He heals the brokenhearted and binds up their wounds" (Psalm 147:3).

Relief From Grief. "So with you: Now is your time of grief, but I will see you again and you will rejoice, and no one will take away your joy" (John 16:22).

Mercy & Grace. "For we do not have a high priest who is unable to empathize with our weaknesses, but we have one who has been tempted in every way, just as we are—yet he did not sin. Let us then approach God's throne of grace with confidence, so that we may receive mercy and find grace to help us in our time of need" (Hebrews 4:15-16).

What if we know God's will, but it involves another person? People were given freewill by God—the choice to follow his ways or to reject them. Therefore, the effectiveness of our prayers that others would change is limited by the willingness of that person. Though God will not change someone against their will, God will provide us with what we need to get through circumstances regarding that person—peace, wisdom, strength. And in some cases, when we ask God to change someone else, we find he changes us.

Focusing on these promises of God will change your life. I encourage you to take one promise at a time and pray it regularly and faithfully, fully expecting to receive it. God's promises never fail.

Reflection: Look through the list of promises above. What promise speaks to your heart right now? Make a reminder for yourself—sticky note, phone alarm, ink on your hand—to pray these specific promises throughout the day.

Prayer: God, thank you that your Word is clear, your promises are true, your gifts are perfect, and I can expect them in your perfect timing when I ask for them. Thank you for making clear what you are longing to give me. I know you choose not to change people against their will, and you don't always change our circumstances, but I'm asking for [Choose one of the promises above and claim it over your life.] I ask these things according to your will. Amen.

Worship: "Promises Never Fail" by Bethel Music and "Yes And Amen" by Jesus Culture

84

Inner Beauty

Your beauty should not come from outward adornment, such as elaborate hairstyles and the wearing of gold jewelry or fine clothes. Rather, it should be that of your inner self, the unfading beauty of a gentle and quiet spirit, which is of great worth in God's sight.

1 Peter 3:3-4

Society's standards for physical beauty are posted everywhere we look—television, billboards, magazines, mannequins, and social media. We are bombarded with these not-so-subliminal lies we buy into: the perfect body gives us worth, an expensive suit brings us success, a gorgeous face gets us the attention we crave. Attaining this standard of beauty is exhausting and, for most of us, impossible and self-destructive in every sense—emotionally, spiritually, and sometimes physically. In these verses, we are instructed to stand firm by refusing to submit to the standards of beauty set by the culture in which we live. We are reminded that true beauty is found, not in our bodies, but in a gentle, quiet spirit.

It is not wrong to dress nicely, wear make-up and jewelry, or style our hair. In fact, I would guess those around us are grateful we put some effort into our appearance. It is the excessive focus on our outer appearance, and neglect of our inner, that becomes harmful. If we do not have the "unfading beauty of a gentle and quiet spirit," no amount of primping will compensate. If we focus only on "outward adornment," we will have only the beauty that attracts the coveted turn of heads, which is a fading beauty, and we will miss the "unfading beauty... which is of great worth in God's sight."

The same Maker who created you also created every colorful sunset, the majestic mountains, and each stunning red rose. He is the mastermind of beauty. Therefore, we can take his word for it when he tells us the thing that is "of great worth in God's sight," and the thing that makes us beautiful is a gentle and quiet spirit.

A gentle spirit is powerfully attractive! Have you ever thought someone was attractive until they opened their mouth, revealing their harsh opinions, causing their beauty to disintegrate into thin air? On the other hand, have you ever met a "Plain Jane" or "Dull Paul" whose gentle and quiet presence drew you in? Consider the state of your spirit. Strive not to be the always elusive "eye candy," but rather a feast for the soul.

Reflection: In what ways do you focus too much on your appearance? Is your self-esteem/confidence dependent upon your looks? Do you have a gentleness about you that attracts authentic, genuine friendships? Do you strive to have the quiet spirit that allows others room to be around you? Is pursuing these attributes a priority to you?

Prayer: God, you are the mastermind of beauty. Thank you for making me beautiful in your sight. Forgive me for putting too much emphasis on my outer appearance. I pray my focus would be on the inner beauty that you promise is unfading. Help me to accept *your* standard of beauty, to find love and acceptance, not from my appearance, but in my amazing worth to you. Develop in me a gentle, quiet spirit. Amen.

Worship: "Beauty Mark" by Natalie Grant and "Image Of God" by We Are Messengers

85

How to Achieve Inner Beauty

Your beauty should not come from outward adornment, such as elaborate hairstyles and the wearing of gold jewelry or fine clothes. Rather, it should be that of your inner self, the unfading beauty of a gentle and quiet spirit, which is of great worth in God's sight.

1 Peter 3:3-4

The attitudes and demeanors of those around us are contagious. We sometimes forget that we, for that matter, affect other people's moods as well. We can overpower the sunny spirit in the room with the dark cloud we bring, or we can warm the air instead with a gentle and quiet spirit. Think of someone in your life whose very presence makes you feel tense and stressed. Think of someone who makes you feel at peace simply because they are at peace and radiate that peace to those around them. The difference is the beauty within the heart. This beauty has nothing to do with the looks we were born with. This beauty is a choice we make. What spirit are we choosing to diffuse in the room?

Consider these scenarios: Bree creates drama everywhere she goes. She only has negative things to say about absolutely everyone. People dread her presence as they often get sucked into her nasty gossip despite their attempts to guide conversations away. People know as soon as they leave the room, they are her next victim. Gina never has anything negative to say about anyone, always giving others the benefit of the doubt. You know when you walk out of the room, your reputation is safe with Gina. All laughter dies down when Jerry walks in a room as people prepare for the onslaught of cynicism about to be rained down. Jess lifts the mood with her charisma and lively personality. Carl causes others to feel as if the world is ending, there's only doom in the future. Carson, with his compassion and gentle spirit, helps others see a way through their seemingly hopeless struggle.

Maybe you want to be less like Bree, Jerry, and Carl and more like Gina, Jess, and Carson. Attaining this requires a heart transformation. A quiet spirit is not brought about by simply suppressing a snappy retort or a hot-tempered opinion. Although biting our tongues is a good place to start, the kind of beauty God wants to instill in us comes from a peaceful place of surrender. It's a transformation of the entire heart and thought process, not simply the words we say.

For outward beauty, we might pay big bucks for a haircut and color, wear jewelry and make-up, or buy expensive clothes. However, for inner beauty (heart transformation), we carve out time to be in the presence of him who holds more beauty than our minds can fathom, learn from his life-changing Word, soak in his love and peace as we communicate with him and adopt a slower pace—a pace that leaves enough room for him. Like the small flame of a candle, gentle as a flicker but powerful enough to change an atmosphere, the light of the Spirit within us makes a powerful difference in the world around us. That is the beauty regime that transforms our "looks," blesses others, and is of great worth to God!

Reflection: Do you relate more to Bree, Gina, Jerry, Jess, Carl, or Carson? What are some practical ways you can quiet your spirit and strive for inner beauty? If you were to surrender and allow God to transform your heart, what would that look like for you personally?

Prayer: Thank you, Father God, for your peace which passes understanding despite my circumstances. It is always available to me, waiting for me to sponge it in and percolate it out. Please teach me to rest in and soak-in your peace. Instill in me a gentle and loving spirit. May I light up every atmosphere I enter. Amen.

Worship: "Change In The Making" by Addison Road and "In Green Pastures" by Jaci Velasquez

86

The Advantage of Overlooking Insults

Fools show their annoyance at once, but the prudent overlook an insult.

PROVERBS 12:16

Kids argue about the most absurd things. Eight-year-old Johnny starts mocking his twelve-year-old sister, Sarah. What happens when Sarah responds by yelling at him to stop? Johnny realizes he has the power to cause a big reaction in his sister, and he likes it! The bickering then continues relentlessly. However, let's say Sarah discovers she can contain the situation by "overlooking the insult." Instead of responding harshly, she ignores him. After a couple more pokes from Johnny with no response from Sarah, Johnny becomes bored by the show of indifference and gives up.

So here we are, as Johnnys and Sarahs several decades later, despite years of opportunities to mature, still falling into this trap of becoming annoyed by "pokes," unable to overlook an offense. Someone grumbles a snide remark with intentions of hurting us. Then, we strike back like a startled cat feeling threatened by a dog.

Sarah learned a better way. By withholding the expected emotional response, she can take away the power of the punch. Holding back a counterattack shows great strength—more strength than the knee-jerk reactions that typically fly out of our mouths. The mature person responds to insults cautiously, knowing the power he holds—power to either take the heat out of the moment or allow the situation to go down in flames.

Not only can we contain the back-and-forth bickering, we can contain the hurt within our hearts. We can prevent those insulting "pokes" from eating away at us. Sometimes we let the harsh, hurtful words settle into our souls, inviting them to destroy us on the inside. But it would do us well to let the insults roll off and, instead, touch base with God for our worth.

Reflection: In what area of life do you allow others to get a rise out of you—with family, at work, while driving, in parenting? Consider ways to keep the situation from escalating, in both your outward response and in your heart regarding your self-worth.

Prayer: Father, forgive me for allowing my emotions to rule my responses to others. Bring healing to the areas of my life I ruined with my angry retorts. Help me to be wise and cautious even when I can feel rage welling inside. Help me to be a peacemaker in my workplace, with my family, while driving, and with my kids. May your gentleness take over my life. Amen.

Worship: "More Heart, Less Attack" by NEEDTOBREATHE and "Turn This Around" by Downhere

87

How to Overlook the Insult

Fools show their annoyance at once, but the prudent overlook an insult.

PROVERBS 12:16

Though we don't have control over many situations we face, we do have control over the way we respond to others. This verse tells us we are wise to overlook a personal attack. Why? Our responses influence many areas in our lives—on the job, with family, within a marriage, with friends, while driving, and in parenting.

Often, our responses have repercussions long into the future, whether positive or negative. In the workplace, responding to an insult may create drama, giving the impression to our boss and coworkers that we are neither professional nor a good team member. In a marriage, our quick responses have incredible power to set the direction of a simple disagreement or, after developing into habit, an entire marriage. With a quick retort, we can embed insecurity and dysfunction. However, with restraint, we can promote strength, trust, and security. Among family members or friends, we can choose peace by diffusing tension and letting spiteful comments roll off. In parenting, training children is more fruitful when negative emotions aren't displayed by the parent. Anger and yelling cause the child's anxiety to increase which is not an optimal state for children to learn.

So how do we control the tongue when we feel our blood start to boil? Here are some simple ways, in the heat of anger, to tame the rabid dog clawing its way out of our mouths:

- Deep breaths. According to multiple studies, deep breathing increases the supply of oxygen to the brain, stimulating the parasympathetic nervous system, and promoting a state of calm. Take in a deep breath, then let it out slowly. Repeat.

- Don't sweat the small stuff. Don't give the minor stressors a room for rent in your head. Evict `em! Save your headspace for the thoughts worthy of your attention.
- In the brief moment of deciding how to respond, envision a good outcome, then consider what needs to happen to get to that point.
- Let go of your desire to fix others, especially your spouse. Remember if you're married, you said, "I do," not "I re-do." Allow people to be who they are without improvements custom-designed by you.
- Keep your esteem dependent on God. The one who is not consumed with proving his worth to others is the one who can ignore the insult. A truly humble person is not thinking of himself at all, but instead concerned about pleasing God alone. That person who truly understands he is the one Jesus would "leave the ninety-nine" for is the person who has no need for a sharp retort to prove his worth.

Reflection: In what area of life do you quickly show your annoyance? What recent situation could have had a better ending if you had chosen to let it go? Which of the above life lessons will you begin working on today?

Prayer: Father, though I don't have control over some of my situations, I realize I do have some control as my responses decide the direction of many situations. I pray I would not be known as a hot-tempered individual with quick, hurtful retorts, but as a wise person who uses words with caution. May I let hurtful comments roll off and depend only on you for my worth. You hold me in high regard, and I pray I can fully grasp what that means. Thank you in advance for the work you're doing in me. Amen.

Worship: "Every Little Prison (Deliver Me)" by Matt Maher, "May The Words" by Ellie Holcomb, and "Let It Roll" by Group 1 Crew

88

The Top of Jesus's Wish List

On coming to the house, they saw the child with his mother Mary, and they bowed down and worshiped him. Then they opened their treasures and presented him with gifts of gold, frankincense and myrrh.

MATTHEW 2:11

Gift giving is the American way to celebrate birthdays, but it's not just the American way. The wise men set an exemplary practice when they brought Jesus gifts in honor of his birth into the human world. They brought tangible gifts to give to their tangible Lord. We no longer have a tangible Lord. He's risen and transcended! So, how do we give gifts to the one without skin? What "treasures" do we have to give? What gift would thrill his heart?

Ephesians 5:10 tells us to find out what pleases God. Fortunately, we don't have to wonder what gifts will please him or take a stab in the dark. He's not the wife who won't give a gift idea because she wants you to guess and then is disappointed when you get it wrong. Jesus has made clear what he treasures.

At the top of his "wish list"? He wants our *love*. In Mark 12:30, Jesus replies to the question, "Of all the commandments, which is the most important?" He reveals his top desire: that we love with everything we have in us. Jesus says, "Love the Lord your God with all your heart and with all your soul and with all your mind and with all your strength." To desire him first above all else, to align our desires with his desires, and to pursue him with every last drop of strength we have.

Number two on his wish list is that we *love others* (Mark 12:31). One way to love others is to serve them, especially those whom society has deemed "the least of these," those with nothing to give back. In Matthew 25:34-40, Jesus says:

> Then the King will say to those on his right, "Come, you who are blessed by my Father; take your inheritance, the kingdom prepared

> for you since the creation of the world. For I was hungry and you gave me something to eat, I was thirsty and you gave me something to drink, I was a stranger and you invited me in, I needed clothes and you clothed me, I was sick and you looked after me, I was in prison and you came to visit me."
>
> Then the righteous will answer him, "Lord, when did we see you hungry and feed you, or thirsty and give you something to drink? When did we see you a stranger and invite you in, or needing clothes and clothe you? When did we see you sick or in prison and go to visit you?"
>
> The King will reply, "Truly I tell you, whatever you did for one of the least of these brothers and sisters of mine, you did for me."

What we do for others, we do for Jesus. These acts of merciful service to others are "gold" to God.

He wants our *quality time*. Luke 10:38-42 recounts an impressionable story:

> As Jesus and his disciples were on their way, he came to a village where a woman named Martha opened her home to him. She had a sister called Mary, who sat at the Lord's feet listening to what he said. But Martha was distracted by all the preparations that had to be made. She came to him and asked, "Lord, don't you care that my sister has left me to do the work by myself? Tell her to help me!"
>
> "Martha, Martha," the Lord answered, "you are worried and upset about many things, but few things are needed—or indeed only one. Mary has chosen what is better, and it will not be taken away from her."

In our achievement-focused society, it's easy to base our worth on our accomplishments, especially for the Christian in the context of serving in the church. In fact, we are called to serve. But it's easy to slip into the mode of keeping "busy" for Jesus and forget he values greater our quality time and attention to him. Jesus would be well-pleased with the gift of regular "visits" with him. He wants for us, like Mary, to be still before him, to listen to him, and to learn from him. He loves the present of our presence.

Reflection: What would it look like for you, personally, to love God with all your heart, soul, and strength? Who in your life is viewed by society as "the least of these" with nothing to give back? Consider giving your time and resources to them as a gift to God. How can you offer your presence to God more consistently?

Prayer: God, I'm so grateful I don't have to scratch my head and wonder what's on your wish list. I pray my life would be a gift to you as a reflection of my gratitude for the ultimate gift you gave me. Thank you for coming to earth in the most humble form to show us how to serve and love, and ultimately to save us. Show me who is in need and how I might serve them. Help me to prioritize my time to give you the gift you truly desire from me, my undivided attention. Amen.

Worship: "Intimacy" by Jonathan David & Melissa Helser and "Move Your Heart" by Upperroom

89

Other Gifts on Jesus's Wish List

On coming to the house, they saw the child with his mother Mary, and they bowed down and worshiped him. Then they opened their treasures and presented him with gifts of gold, frankincense and myrrh.

MATTHEW 2:11

Just as the wise men brought gifts to celebrate Jesus's entrance into our world, we too can bring him gifts fit for a King. In the previous devotion, we learned Jesus desires for us to love him, love one another, and spend time in his presence. Let's consider the many other gifts on his wish list.

He wants *recognition* and our *adoration* (Psalm 68:4, Jeremiah 20:13, 1 Chronicles 16:34, Colossians 3:16). At the end of a performance, we give applause, showing our enjoyment of the performance. If the praise that's due through applause isn't given, things get awkward. When credit is given to the wrong artist for a painting as the true artist is brushed aside and disregarded, that is a travesty. Romans 1:25 says, "They exchanged the truth about God for a lie, and worshiped and served created things rather than the Creator—who is forever praised." Basically, they disregard the Artist to bow down to the canvas. Credit is given to the painting as if it painted itself! The earth's beauty, the complexity of the human body, and miracles that take place are just a few of the magnificent wonders we oftentimes don't take the time to give credit where it's due.

Praise—giving gratitude—is one of the highest gifts we can give. We don't feed our children, clean up their messes, and help them with their homework for the purpose of receiving the recognition. We do it because we love them and want the best for them. However, neither do we like to be taken for granted. We love when our children appreciate the sacrifices and good things we give them. Much the same, God loves our gratitude. Not only that, God created us to praise him and it is in that place—where we are giving credit to him—we feel most fulfilled. John Piper says, "The reason God seeks our supreme praise, or that Jesus seeks our supreme love, is not because he's needy and won't be fully God until he gets it, but because we are needy and won't be fully happy until we give it."[9]

Another gift God loves to receive is our *sacrifice* (Hebrews 13:16, Romans 12:1, 1 Peter 2:5). Sacrifice isn't giving away our excess that we aren't going to use anyway. Sacrifice takes something away from us causing us to feel a discomfort with its loss. Jesus expressed in Mark 12:42-44, the one who gave only a few cents, though it's all she had, gave more than those who donated large amounts out of their wealth. Jesus showed his love to us through a great sacrifice, and loves when we, in return, sacrifice for him.

But even more than our sacrifice, Jesus desires our *obedience* (1 Samuel 15:22-23, Proverbs 21:3). He says in John 14:15, "If you love me, keep my commands." He reiterates it again in verse 21, "Whoever has my commands and keeps them is the one who loves me. The one who loves me will be loved by my Father, and I too will love them and show myself to them." Although obedience is not our way to salvation (that is through grace alone, according to Ephesians 2:8), submitting our own will to obey him is a great way to show God we love him. And it always works out best for us in the end! See 1 John 5:2-3, 1 John 2:3-6, and Psalm 119:1-8.

Jesus desires our *skills* and *abilities* to be used for his glory. In Matthew 25:14-30, he tells us he wants us to invest our talents. The fictitious Little Drummer Boy exemplifies this in the popular Christmas carol. The Little Drummer Boy felt he had nothing to give that was "fit for a King," so he did what he knew and played his drum to the best of his ability. Using our talents God gifted us, we can use them as a gift to glorify him—to "play" our "best for him."

Reflection: What are you most grateful for when you think of all Jesus has done for you? Do you bring him praise regularly, or only on Sundays? Consider making it a habit to thank him throughout the day every time you are aware of his provision. Do you give only what is excess, or does your giving cause a little discomfort? In what ways could you be more obedient to him? What talent has God given you that you could invest further to bring the glory back to him?

Prayer: God, thank you for saving me, providing for me, rescuing me from pits I've fallen into, and for working things out for my good. Forgive me when I don't give credit where credit is due. Help me to walk in obedience. Sometimes my way seems better to me, and I forget your ways are higher. Help me to always remember that your ways may be more challenging but always lead to abundance. I pray you would make me aware of the talents you gifted to me and show me ways I can give that talent back to you. Amen.

Worship: "All I Am" by Phil Wickham and "Gratitude" by Brandon Lake

90

Surely, Not Everything, Right?

In the same way, those of you who do not give up everything you have cannot be my disciples.

LUKE 14:33

What?! Jesus wants me to give up everything I have? By the time Jesus made this far-reaching statement, he had quite the following. Large crowds had been tagging along with him as he traveled, curious and captivated, but not committed. Jesus wanted to make clear to them, before they decided to follow him, the cost of being his disciple was steep: they would have to give up everything they had.

Disciple means learner. To learn from Jesus means more than merely listening to a sermon. Learning requires action. The action? Sacrifice. Jesus knew there were people in the crowd following him simply because he inspired them. They weren't there for the life change. He gave thought-provoking messages, offered healing for incurable diseases, and granted forgiveness and salvation to those hungry for hope. For many following him then (and for some of us today), it was solely about what he could do for them, about miracles, about attaining blessings for themselves. To be a true follower of Jesus meant something more, something most people didn't (and still don't) bargain for. His way goes deeper, requiring sacrifice and commitment, an extreme and transformational investment.

How extreme an investment? Everything. Every. Single. Thing.

One might think, after reading this verse, Jesus requires us to sell everything we own, and leave our families, to follow him. But when we look at the story of Zacchaeus, we see Zacchaeus decided to give half of everything he had to the poor and to pay back four times the amount he had cheated the people. That was enough for Jesus to reach and change Zacchaeus. And, although Levi "left everything and followed him," we are then told Levi "held a great banquet for Jesus at his house" (Luke 5:27-29). Apparently, Levi didn't give up his house but was still considered a follower. In addition, we find many of the disciples who followed Jesus retained some of their possessions. John took Jesus's mother into his home after the crucifixion (John 19:27). A few of the disciples were using their boats and nets to fish when Jesus appeared to them following the resurrection (John 21:1-14).

Clearly, Jesus didn't intend for us to literally get rid of everything we own. So, what did he mean? We can conclude Jesus was speaking about priorities. We are being called to part with anything that gets in our way of serving him. We should be ready, whenever he may call, to sacrifice anything and everything for his sake. We can hold nothing too tightly but come to him with open hands. "Giving up everything" means when God asks it of us, at the drop of a hat, we give without hesitation, unhindered and unconstrained.

God wants top priority in our lives. He is jealous for us when we put anything before him (Exodus 20:5). Whether it be money, material possessions, relationships, or our plans. If anything becomes more important than his place in our lives or hinders our growing relationship with him, then it needs to go.

As always, Jesus directs us to look at our hearts. Are we willing to give *all* if it were asked of us? Or are we holding too tightly to the objects we've acquired in this temporary kingdom? What, when you think of sacrificing it, leaves you unsettled and apprehensive? What would be too difficult for you to give up—your dream home, your car, your hobby, entertainment, comfort, an unhealthy habit, a relationship you've prioritized over him, a relationship dragging you away from him, your position in your career…?

Jesus says it is difficult for "someone who is rich" to enter into the Kingdom of Heaven (Matthew 19:24). I imagine this is so because the more we have, the more difficult it is for us when we are asked to let go. Luke 12:48 says for him who is given much, of him much will be demanded. Before you go thinking you aren't in the "much will be demanded" group, if you're American, you are rich. The poorest American is richer than 80 percent of the world.

Though we may feel God demands more than we can give, let's remember: He empowers us to do anything and everything he asks of us. We need only be willing, and he will take our hand and walk with us as we walk those steps out in faith.

Reflection: What are you holding onto a little too tightly? Is there anything you would not be willing to part with? Have you been called to sacrifice something but shrugged it off because it demanded *just too much*? What has Jesus called you to abandon to fully follow him?

Prayer: Savior, sometimes you ask me to sacrifice, but I don't want to let go of my things and my comforts. Forgive me for the times I have prioritized comfort over sacrifice and stagnation over growing in my relationship with you. Help me to reprioritize the things I hold dear. I pray I would hold my things and comforts so loosely that I could toss them aside in an instant with no hesitations. I trust what you have in store for me is worth every sacrifice. Amen.

Worship: "Give My Life Away" by Big Daddy Weave and "Letting Go" by Jeremy Camp

91

Simply Overseers

In the same way, those of you who do not give up everything you have cannot be my disciples.

Luke 14:33

We learned in the previous devotion, we are required to give up everything which includes anything hindering us from learning, growing in our faith, or serving Christ. Anything and everything is on the table as a potential sacrifice. We can have things, but we need to rethink our "ownership" of the things we have. When we follow Christ, not only do we belong to him, everything we "own" is his. That make us simply overseers of the things in our possession.

Most of us would love to keep our comfortable lives and slide God somewhere in the cracks where we are lacking. Or we want to spend our money on "stuff" to improve our lifestyle, and then tithe only whatever is left over. But we can't just add Jesus to our greedy, consumerist lifestyle as a way of taking care of a spiritual need. When we commit our lives to Christ, we really commit everything. The Greek word for *give up* in this verse is *apotassetai*, which means to renounce. As followers of Jesus, we renounce ownership, or surrender the deed, to all we own. We acknowledge that nothing is our own, not even our own spirits or our own bodies (1 Corinthians 6:19-20). He owns it all. We are simply overseers. So, when he asks us to give up something or shift "oversight" of what we "own" to someone else, we must follow his orders.

When my daughter was three years old, she was fighting with her brother over a balloon she received. I told her everything in this world belongs to God, including the balloon, and that even though God lets us use things, he wants us to share them. She took the lesson to heart and easily shared the balloon with her brother. Several hours later, when the conversation was off my mind, the balloon in the next room randomly popped. My daughter gasped in surprise, "That was God's balloon!" I imagine she was bewildered as to why God would want to pop his balloon. May we get to the point where we can say after "our" balloon pops (or a cherished family heirloom breaks, our dream home is lost, our valued material item is loaned to someone in need, our peaceful environment is sacrificed for a ministry, our free time is spent on less-than-gratifying demands), "That is God's, and he can do with it as he chooses."

What are you holding onto with a tight grasp? What would be difficult for you to give up if God nudged you to do so? Here are a few examples to spark your thoughts: your free time on a Saturday to help someone on bedrest, a downsize from the vehicle that has you strapped financially to a car that's not quite the statement you want to make, the use of your home for a church or Bible study gathering, a move into a smaller house in order to reduce debt, a laughter-filled night out with friends to sit instead with a grieving friend, negative self-talk and pity parties for confidence in God, the triumph of winning an argument at the price of another's dignity, a move to a third-world country to help them gain access to clean water and education in agriculture, a new 9:00 bedtime to face the next day with a good attitude, TV time in exchange for reading devotions with the kids, a friend who leads you into temptation, or your favorite music that leads your thoughts astray. If the idea of surrendering any of these suggestions caused a twinge of unease inside you, consider that an area you may be holding too tightly.

A faith that costs nothing is worth nothing. Before we consider "everything" too much to sacrifice, let's remember the prize we win is worth the price we pay. Jesus promises our sacrifices will be repaid one hundred times (Mark 10:28-31). He wants our focus, not on the here-and-now where our things can be taken, destroyed, and left behind, but on the eternal Kingdom (Matthew 6:19-21). And in Matthew 6:33, he tells us when we focus on him and his kingdom, we will have not only a reward in the future, but our needs for the here-and-now met.

You may have seen a popular meme with a picture of a little girl holding a teddy bear and Jesus reaching to take it while she says, "But I love it, God..." Jesus is saying, "Just trust me..." What the girl doesn't see is Jesus holding a larger teddy bear behind his back, ready to give in exchange if she would just let go of that small bear. I can't tell you what he's asking of you—that is for you alone to learn. But we can't know if we don't tune in to him, learn his heart, learn his ways, and pray for clarification on what he wants of us. We must be willing to let go of the life we thought we wanted for his promise of something better.

Reflection: Would you consider God to be the Lord over your finances and possessions? What, when you think of it being taken from you, causes anxiety in you? Have you felt a prompting to give up something, or to use something you "own," for God's glory? How is your life a reflection of what you have given up for God? Do you think others see your pursuit of Jesus as top priority over everything?

Prayer: Proprietor of my life and everything I own, I relinquish the deed to all that I have. I simply want to be the overseer of the things you have placed in my care. Please make clear to me your will for the things I oversee. Change my heart until I view the relationship I have with my things in the light it should be viewed. I pray nothing in my clutch would hinder my growth or your glory. Amen.

Worship: "Kingdom of Comfort" by Delirious? and "Heart Abandoned" by Passion

92

Reckless Zeal

For where you have envy and selfish ambition, there you find disorder and every evil practice.

James 3:16

"All kids should be homeschooled."

"Kids should never be homeschooled."

"People who eat meat have no compassion."

"Drug addicts should not receive welfare."

"Teenagers wouldn't be doing drugs if they had good parents."

"Moms of young kids should not work outside the home."

We are not in short supply of opinions surrounding us! Hopefully, before forming an opinion, we are considering all angles, and afterward, continually keeping our minds open to views other than our own.

Have you ever met someone who is so preoccupied with his own view, it's beyond the bounds of possibility for him to *see* the view of anyone else? These kinds of people push and push their viewpoints, not stopping until their objector rolls over in defeat, pretends to agree, or worse, relationships are broken.

It is necessary to dive into the Greek to fully understand this verse because the words *envy* and *selfish ambition* don't give the full picture of the original Greek words. The Greek word used here that most versions of the Bible translate to *envy* is *zēlos,* which is defending anything indignantly and contentiously. It is related to the word *zealot*—obsessed and fanatical about one's beliefs. The Greek word for *selfish ambition* is *eritheia,* which is acting for personal gain, regardless if it causes another strife. With these definitions in mind, we get the picture of one who is so preoccupied with his own ideas, he can't or won't consider anyone else's viewpoint. Not only is he preoccupied with his own opinions, he feels compelled to set the world straight as they are "sadly erroneous." It may feel good to win an argument or change another's opinion through coercion, but chaos follows intensely opinionated people. They leave a trail of ruined, broken relationships. The Word calls it evil. This is not insignificant. It is ugly.

Respectfully sharing our opinions is okay. It's not okay to keep someone locked in our "pushy prisons." If we keep pushing our opinions, even after we've already made them known, it is not likely others will convert to our way of thinking. In fact, pushiness pushes *away*, not *toward*. Likely, we will not change a mind, but destroy a relationship. Whether our opinion is right or wrong, it will not be received if it hasn't been invited.

The Bible commands us to proclaim the truth of God's Word to others (Mark 16:15). The great news, though, is that we're not personally responsible for making others accept truth or for changing their lives! Transforming hearts is the job of the Spirit. We are commanded simply to proclaim truth and to love. Pushiness—reckless zeal—doesn't fit in with love. In fact, it looks a lot like pious contempt. If it lacks love or respect, it lacks effect. You might be right, but even if you're a prophet, Paul says without love you're just a clanging cymbal (1 Corinthians 13:1). Next time you are tempted to beat your opinion into someone, picture yourself as a clanging cymbal for that is what will be heard.

In 2 Timothy 2:24-25, we read how to approach those who oppose our views: "And the Lord's servant must not be quarrelsome but must be kind to everyone, able to teach, not resentful. Opponents must be gently instructed, in the hope that God will grant them repentance leading them to a knowledge of the truth." Sometimes others are enlightened by our views, and sometimes they reject them. No matter the outcome, it's important to keep our relationships alive and healthy. Next time you give an opinion, first ask yourself some questions: Am I being argumentative? Am I being kind? Is my response gentle? Am I communicating truth well? Do I resent this person? Does this person know I love them? Using these questions as filters goes a long way in preserving relationships.

Although we are called to tell others the truth of God's Word, there are areas the Bible is silent. In those areas, our opinions need to be held loosely. We must always extend grace to others and give space for free thought. Confining differences is not love.

Are we, ourselves, open to listening and considering the other side? Are we open to a change in thinking? Many times, after researching and deciding something to be truth, we then "set that truth in stone." We don't make room for the ideas, thoughts, and opinions of others. Are we too prideful to admit we may have been wrong? Or are we afraid of the actual truth? If it is in fact true, we don't have to be afraid of it. Open-mindedness does not mean we are wishy washy, spineless, or weak. It means we are wise and mature enough to make room for growth.

Reflection: Have you ever felt so sure about something, only to be proven wrong? How did you respond to being wrong? Do you feel like you consider, and even value, your family's, friend's, and/or spouse's thoughts and opinions? When you have felt compelled to share an opinion or truth, have you done so according to 2 Tim. 2:22-25, pursuing peace with kindness and gentleness, not resentment? Are there those in your life with whom you need to make amends due to your reckless zeal?

Prayer: Father, forgive me when I don't listen well to others and become the source of strife. Help me to be respectful when I disagree and to make room for the thoughts and opinions of others. Give me wisdom to discern correctly and the ability to make others feel valued, even when I don't agree. Please help me to keep my relationships intact despite differing opinions. Amen.

Worship: "Right With You" by Big Daddy Weave and "Greatest Of These" by Hillsong UNITED

93

Unity of Mind

Finally, all of you, have unity of mind, sympathy, brotherly love, a tender heart, and a humble mind.

1 Peter 3:8 esv

When a Christian bad-mouths, snubs, or argues against a fellow Christian, what does that say about Christianity? What does it say about the one whom we serve? What if, instead, we acted unified, sympathetic, tender hearted, and humble? What if we showed brotherly love unconditionally, and put others above ourselves at all times?

How can we have "unity of mind" when we're all created with different strengths, different qualities, and different personalities? Some of us were given strong wills, while some find surrender easy. Some of us are driven by high ambitions, while some are content and easy-going. Some of us are born leaders, while some are drawn to another's cause. Although, God made us all so different from one another, he still wants us to have unity of mind. This doesn't mean we have identical thoughts and ways of doing things. Rather, it is like we are an orchestra, all playing to the beat of the same drum. Though we all play different instruments, different notes, even at different times and volumes, we are unified in our goal and purpose, creating one beautiful, harmonious song.

There's something wondrous about Christianity. Once we make that commitment to trust Jesus, the Spirit moves in. That's phenomenal, in itself, but it gets even better! The Spirit within us recognizes the same Spirit in others. It becomes distinctly evident when traveling to another country or meeting new believers from a different culture or language. Though we can't communicate verbally, the Spirit within each of us communicates in a deeper, more profound way than spoken language. In Christianity, "strangers" become family with one vision and mission. (If you have the Spirit and you have never gone to church in another country, I highly recommend it. When your Spirit connects with another for no reason apparent to you, it is faith-solidifying!)

Unity is important to God. "How good and pleasant it is when God's people live together in unity!" we read in Psalm 133:1. Paul recognized unity as essential. He wrote in another letter: "Make every effort to keep the unity of the Spirit through the bond of peace" (Ephesians 4:3). Unity should be important to us as well. How do we keep the unity when we all have different ideas and views, even different perceptions of the same Scriptures? Even Paul didn't see eye-to-eye with every believer. He had a sharp disagreement with Barnabas, his friend and partner in ministry. They had to "agree to disagree" and go their separate ways (Acts 15:39). When differences cannot be agreed upon, moving on is better than disunity. When Paul and Barnabas parted ways, God carried the mission on through each of them and the gospel continued to spread.

For further instruction on keeping unity, Paul spells it out clearly: "Be completely humble and gentle; be patient, bearing with one another in love" (Ephesians 4:2). The New Living Translation puts it this way "...making allowance for each other's faults because of your love." We cover others in the grace we ourselves have been covered. Our attitude should be, *I make mistakes too. I love you even still.*

Christians are bound by duty to be known for love and unity. So let's unify.

Reflection: Have you witnessed non-believers repulsed by Christianity due to dissension among Christians? What could have been said or done differently by the Christians for the sake of unity? Have you ever felt the sense of "family" among Christians? Think about your church, fellowship with other believers and your marriage. Do you have unity of mind? Despite your differences, are you marching to the beat of the same drum? What could you do to better attain unity?

Prayer: Thank you, God, for your Spirit we share among us. I pray you would teach us to have unity within our church, among other believers, and within our family. Help me to cooperate with the natural unity that comes when the Spirit within me touches the Spirit within my fellow Christ follower. May we be indivisible, though we have different ideas on how to complete your missions. Unify us in the decisions we make, the outreach we do, programs we put together, and the way we interact with one another. May we work well together, bringing our differences into one beautiful song for you. Amen.

Worship: "Sing" by Sanctus Real and "They'll Know We Are Christians By Our Love" by Jars Of Clay

94

Sympathy, Brotherly Love, Tender Heart

Finally, all of you, have unity of mind, sympathy, brotherly love, a tender heart, and a humble mind.

1 Peter 3:8 ESV

What does compassion feel like? It's the feeling we get when we see someone struggling in a difficult situation—physically, mentally, or emotionally—which causes in us a desire to do something to ease their suffering. Sometimes we feel the emotions of others when we're not in their situation.

Brotherly love comes from the Greek word *philadelphoi, sympathy* from the Greek word, *sympathies,* and *tender heart* from *eusplanchnoi.* All three words point to unity of minds accomplished through compassion, sympathizing, and brotherly love. Compassion means to suffer together, as such, it brings unity by an odd means—through suffering.

It is clear God wants us to have sympathy for one another. He wants us to rejoice with those who rejoice and mourn with those who mourn (Romans 12:15). The opposite—to feel callous, cold, and aloof—is not Christ-like. Even *Jesus wept,* demonstrating his compassion for Mary who was grieving the loss of her brother, Lazarus. John 11:33 tells us, "He was deeply moved in spirit and troubled." If we are to be like him, then we will be moved by others' sorrow and joy. We must first have awareness of the pain of others, then allow our hearts to be moved, and finally, act on that compassion. Jesus simply "feeling" something for Mary wasn't the entirety of Jesus's sympathy. The compassion Jesus expressed was a compassion that drove him to act. When his emotions shifted, he did something about it. He raised this heart-broken woman's brother from the dead.

The family of Christians is a support system. We are called to live as a community that comforts, supports, and encourages during the hard times, and celebrates others' victories. We have enough suffering all around us. We are all wounded. The community of Christ should not be where further wounds are created, but instead healed.

My daughter had a fever for 11 weeks. My other daughter would go out and play with the neighbors each day while my daughter with sickness watched from inside. Ava, our next-door neighbor, had sympathy for my daughter who was stuck inside so long. So, she decided to be a "secret friend." She began leaving gifts and letters on the porch for my stuck-inside daughter. She did what Jesus commanded and put her compassion into action.

Compassion without action leaves us feeling empty. So, let's follow Jesus's example—take that compassion we feel for another, let it move us in spirit, and then move us to action.

Reflection: Have you experienced the tender-heartedness of another in a time of need? When was the last time you were "deeply moved in spirit and troubled" over another's pain? In what practical way can you put your compassion into action?

Prayer: Father, sometimes I get so caught up in my own world, I feel I have nothing left to give to another's world. Please, help me to notice the pain around me. Move my spirit by others' joy and pain. May I celebrate their victories with them and act to alleviate their sorrow. Give me wisdom and creativity when I feel "moved and troubled in spirit" but am unsure what to do. Amen.

Worship: "My Own Little World" by Matthew West, and "The Power Of Your Name" by Lincoln Brewster

95

The Humble Mind

Finally, all of you, have unity of mind, sympathy, brotherly love, a tender heart, and a humble mind.

1 Peter 3:8 esv

Kanye West, a man once full of pride, has said, "I am the number one most impactful artist of our generation."[10] Moreover, he said his greatest pain in life was that he would never be able to see himself perform live. Kanye was a man full of himself. However, after giving his life to Christ, he began to portray a very different man. In his song, "Hands On," he sings that he deserves criticism and has been changed to a man who praises God. He goes from believing he's the best to begging for prayer, laying down his pride, and identifying himself as a man who knows he's in need of grace. The humility is admirable.

Humility means we are willing to take a "lower place" when given the opportunity for a higher position. Humility usually gets a bad rap. It sometimes gets associated with weakness, shame, timidity, and incapability. However, humility is a sign of great strength! When we earn first place, yet choose to allow others to have it, or when the spotlight is on us and we use it to raise up another, it displays incredible strength of mind and will.

Do we admire those who are pushy and self-assertive, desiring power and position over others? Or do we naturally respect those who choose modesty in spirit? People in all cultures tend to establish a "pecking order." Ironically, when we pridefully push ourselves to the top of the pecking order, we are sorely disappointed as others' respect for us drops.

Take this 20-question "humility test" to determine if you're a humble person or if you could stand to knock your pride down a few notches:

- I can easily acknowledge I don't have it all together.

- I'm okay if others get the credit that belongs to me.
- I put effort into building up others.
- I don't feel a need to defend myself because others' opinions don't define my worth.
- I don't feel a need to tell others about my accomplishments.
- I can continue driving peacefully when a "backseat driver" is telling me to slow down or to take a different route.
- I don't want others to view me as a victim.
- I'm completely open to correction.
- Instead of giving others a "piece of my mind," I can easily say, *Maybe I don't have all the answers, but here are my thoughts for whatever they're worth.*
- I love to cheer others on even when they're ahead of me.
- People who live their lives differently than me don't annoy me. I can easily continue interactions with them.
- I live below my means, in moderation.
- I allow others to choose the restaurants, movies, plans for business actions, and other details.
- I don't look down on others based on the contents in their grocery cart, the clothes they wear, their body shape, their careers, their political views, or their life choices.
- It's okay if I'm seen in public not looking my best.
- I ask others if they want my opinion before offering it to them.
- I am content to listen to another's story without feeling an urge to one-up them with a story of my own.
- When I'm given an important position, I realize it's not because I'm better than others.
- I cannot say there is one person I have not forgiven.
- I realize I still have a lot to learn.

How did we do on the humility test? I'm guessing most of us, myself included, realized we're not as humble as we thought we were. And if we did pass the humility test with flying colors, we may want to check again!

Humility leads us back to unity of mind because we "play well with others." Humility allows sympathy, brotherly love, and a tender heart to guide our lives into unity in community.

Reflection: Read through the humility test again—slowly and prayerfully. Highlight the statements you can't say about yourself without doubt. What is God pointing out to you and how will you respond?

Prayer: God, I realize I am not as a humble a person as I originally thought. Please take away any desire within me to prove myself to others, to look down on others, and [list other areas you struggle with]. Help me to find my confidence and contentment with who I am in you. May my humility lead to compassion and brotherly love. Help me to see others the way you see them. Amen.

Worship: "Weak Man" by Leeland and "Broken" by Lincoln Brewster

96

No Retaliation

Don't repay evil for evil. Don't retaliate with insults when people insult you. Instead, pay them back with a blessing. That is what God has called you to do, and he will grant you his blessing.

1 Peter 3:9 NLT

My neighbor was having an in-ground swimming pool built in his backyard. Another neighbor, irritated by the loud noise of the construction vehicles during the day, decided at 10:00 p.m. to run his lawn mower up and down the sidewalk of pool-building neighbor to "retaliate" for the noise. This is a ridiculous example of retaliation. However, there are countless hard-core, even disturbing accounts of vengeance. I'm sure you know of some horrific examples yourself. Vengeance never goes well, not for the victim nor for the one seeking revenge, and never brings about positive change. Nothing good comes from revenge…ever.

Revenge isn't found just among neighbors. It has found its way into our homes, workplaces, and friendships. *You yell at me; I'll yell back at you. You won't fix the broken doorknob, then I won't do your laundry. You won't help me around the house, then I won't sleep with you. You didn't invite me to your New Year's Eve party, so I won't invite you to my Superbowl party. You didn't cover for me at work, so I'll never cover for you again.* To all my Christian peeps out there, we cannot live like this! Our relationships will not survive. Our community will not survive.

When someone wrongs us, it is not within our nature to "let it go." Naturally, we want them to pay. So, giving in to what feels natural, we step down into the muck to enter their game and the downward spiral begins. We think revenge will relieve our anger; however, that's not the way it works. Building our happiness on someone else's unhappiness is backward. Revenge doesn't bring us the happiness or freedom we thought, in our moment of anger, that it would.

The only way to arrive at genuine peace and happiness is to break the cycle of revenge and forgive.

Acknowledging our pain, for a moment, can be beneficial, but then we must leave it behind through prayer. If we decide, instead, to feed the serpent of anger and indignation, it grows, coiling around us until it has choked the life out of us. Dwelling in pain and resentment—allowing another's sin to influence the way *we* live—is destructive to our own selves. We must put an end to animosity for it has the power to destroy everything.

Reflection: Consider a time you took revenge on another. How did it end? Consider a time you chose to let go of an offense. How did it end? To whom do you need to extend undeserved grace and forgiveness?

Prayer: Thank you, Father, for forgiving me, over and over. Reveal to me any grudges I am holding. Please help me to let them go. I need your supernatural power to do this as I am unable in my own strength. I know with your Spirit, I am able. Help me to remember it is the best choice I can make for my own life. Amen.

Worship: "Forgiveness" by Matthew West and "Losing" by Tenth Avenue North

97

Payback With a Blessing

Don't repay evil for evil. Don't retaliate with insults when people insult you. Instead, pay them back with a blessing. That is what God has called you to do, and he will grant you his blessing.

1 PETER 3:9 NLT

The Bible not only commands us to forgive those who have wronged us, it goes even further and commands us to pay them back with a blessing! Really?! Someone hurts us and we are to think of a way we can *bless* them?

In the Old Testament, we find many prayers, specifically from David, asking God to destroy his enemies. However, when David was presented with an opportunity, and even urged by his own men, to kill his enemy, David instead spared King Saul's life. David had been running from Saul, living an uncomfortable, nomadic life, hiding in caves, fearing Saul's sword, for years—not days, not months—*years*! Yet, he passed the opportunity to retaliate (1 Samuel 24).

During David's life, the law was "an eye for an eye," paying back aggressions in the same proportion to the offense (Exodus 21:24). Jesus came and turned the law upside-down with grace. Jesus's radical teaching was to love our enemies, pray for them, and bless them.

Blessing in the Greek is *eulogountes*, which conveys speaking well of another. So, this verse tells us we are to speak well of our enemies. Instead of going around telling everyone the ways we've been wronged, we are to protect the reputation of those who have hurt us.

It's not in our nature, or even in our human power, to wish our enemies well. We need the supernatural power of God to *agape** love those who have

* *agape*: There are four words used for *love* in the New Testament. A brotherly/friendship love, *philia*, a romantic love, *eros*, a familial love, *storge*, and *agape*. *Agape* love is a self-sacrificing love that gives without demands or expectations of repayment, not out of pride or for a pat on the back, has little to do with the feeling of love and much to do with self-denial for the sake of another's best interest. *Agape* is awakened when we realize God's love for us.

wronged us. It's the high road. Anyone can love someone who loves them back, but only with the Spirit can we show love to our enemies and give them what they don't deserve—kindness. To give them what we ourselves have received from God—grace.

Paying back heartache with a blessing sounds ludicrous to us, but God sees the big picture and knows how to break the cycle. Although, pursuing peace by blessing those who have wronged us is not in our nature, it's in his who is within us, and it is the only way to freedom.

Many commands in the Bible, including this command, are followed by a blessing. It says in 1 Peter 3:9, when we choose to pay someone back with a blessing instead of retaliation, we will inherit God's blessing. We are promised when we respond to others with gentleness and don't allow anxiety to rule our hearts, we are given peace beyond understanding. Peace that doesn't make sense in our circumstances (Philippians 4:5-7). He promises we will be restored after going through bitter troubles (Psalm 71:20). He gives healing where our hearts have been broken (Psalm 147:3). But that healing cannot reach us until the serpent of resentment dies.

Reflection: In what way have you been wronged? In what ways can you bless your transgressor? Make the decision to not withhold good from that person. Pray for them.

Prayer: Father, thank you for blessing me when I didn't deserve it and for teaching me the way to abundant life. I pray you will bless [insert your enemy's name]. God, I know many times people hurt others from a deep pain within themselves. I pray when [enemy's name] lashes out at me, I wouldn't take it to heart but put my confidence in your love for me. Please heal [enemy's name]—heal their broken spirit so they may be able to experience meaningful relationships. Give them peace and joy. Give me ideas for ways I can bless them instead. Give me the energy to climb over the mountain of my hurt and show them kindness. Amen.

Worship: "Forgiveness" by Beckah Shae and "The Blessing" by Kari Jobe, Elevation Worship or Bethel Music (Sing these words over someone you are offering forgiveness.)

98

The Workmanship

For we are His workmanship, created in Christ Jesus for good works, which God prepared beforehand so that we would walk in them.

Ephesians 2:10 NASB

What an inspiring thought! We are God's workmanship. *Workmanship* comes from the Greek word *poiema*, which is also where we get the word *poem*. Have you ever thought of yourself as a divine work of poetry, a literary treasure that flows with beauty and design, a depiction of the very Creator himself?

Some days, you may feel more like a mess than a masterpiece, but God doesn't make messes. Think of a carefully planned, highly detailed, and beautifully designed cross-stitch. When we look at the underside of a cross-stitch, we see only frayed strings and a knotted conglomeration. However, when we turn it over, we see a design we then comprehend. We see beauty, the workmanship of the artist, the true intention of the design. It was always there but it requires looking at the intended side of the cross-stitch to enlighten us to what it is. In the same way, once we turn over our thought process and align our thoughts with God's truth about ourselves, we then see who we truly are.

Joni Eareckson Tada, a beautiful woman who experienced a tragic accident that left her paralyzed, describes herself as God's *poiema* in her book, *A Place of Healing*. She writes, "[God] has a plan and purpose for my time on earth. He is the Master Artist or Sculptor, and he is the one who chooses the tools he will use to perfect his handiwork. What of suffering, then? What of illness? What of disability? Am I to tell him which tools he can use and which tools he can't use in the lifelong task of perfecting me and molding me into the beautiful image of Jesus? Do I really know better than him, so that I can state without equivocation that it's always his will to heal me of every physical affliction? If I am his poem, do I have the right to say, 'No, Lord. You need to trim line number two and brighten up lines three and five. They're just a little bit dark.' Do I, the poem, the thing being written, know more than the poet?"[11]

We are God's workmanship, created with unique purpose. Sometimes, we'd love to write our own story, to mold ourselves with a gentle, painless chisel. However, we are the created, not the Creator. God is the master craftsman. We are but a toddler with a crayon.

Reflection: What is your response to the idea you are a masterpiece? How hard is it for you to turn the cross-stitch of your life over and realize you are a beautiful masterpiece? If you were to fully believe and remember you are God's workmanship, how would you be living your life differently?

Prayer: Creator, author of my life, thank you for writing every detail of my story, making it beautiful, redeeming the broken parts, healing and making new what once looked like a mess of thread and knots. It's a hard concept for me to grasp that I'm a beautiful work of art as I often feel like a hot mess. I turn over my thoughts to you. May it change my self-talk from negative to positive. May I allow your truth about me to change the way I live. Amen.

Worship: "Scarlet Thread" by JJ Heller, "Write Your Story" by Francesca Battistelli, and "Beautiful Offering" by Big Daddy Weave

99

The Works Prepared Beforehand

For we are His workmanship, created in Christ Jesus for good works, which God prepared beforehand so that we would walk in them.

EPHESIANS 2:10 NASB

Believe it or not, though we are a work of art, we were *not* created simply as an exhibit for display, a painting on a wall, or statue on a shelf. Rather, we were created for a purpose, for action, for "good works." Jesus "went around doing good" when he walked this earth (Acts 10:38). God's plan is that we continue that good work. God wants to show how awesome he is, to demonstrate his glory, his awesome power, and his deep, deep love for all people. His chosen method? *Us!* Crazy to think he wants to use *us* to do his work. We bring joy to our Creator and meaning to our existence when we simply do what he has designed us to do.

God designed these beautiful masterpieces—us—for action. Although we don't always know in advance the actions we were created to carry out, we are told the actions have already been prepared beforehand for us to do. He brings us to these prepared moments and sometimes doesn't equip us until that very moment. As we are led into them, we need to surrender our own resolve and be willing to carry them out with the strength he gives. In doing so, we become a gift back to our Creator.

We may be given *small* tasks throughout our day, such as listening to someone who is hurting, allowing someone who appears hurried to go in front of us in line, giving someone a compliment, running an errand for a friend in need, picking up a chore that our spouse normally undertakes, leaving a generous tip, or saying something kind to our coworker to brighten his or her day. There may be a bit *more* required of us, such as serving at a homeless shelter, teaching a Sunday school class, running a 5K for a good cause, sharing the gospel with someone who is living without hope, standing up for someone who was treated unfairly, committing ourselves to pray for the broken, making dinner for someone in need, buying school supplies and coats for the needy, supporting a missionary, visiting a nursing home, befriending the unlovable, stopping to help someone with a flat tire, making amends with an estranged family member, or forgiving someone for hurting us. There may even be a *grand act of great sacrifice* prepared beforehand, such as babysitting for very little to no pay on a regular basis for a single mom, fostering someone with special needs, turning down a job promising $500K for a ministry position offering only $40K, or putting our own life in danger to rescue victims of human trafficking. No matter the extent of the sacrifice asked of us, when we sense that urging, we shouldn't brush it off. That urging just might be the reason for our life.

Sometimes, we work diligently on these tasks God has prepared beforehand for us to do, but we see no fruit. This can be discouraging; however, seeing the fruit of our labor is not always part of God's plan. We are not called to success by our own standard. We are called to obedience. Many times, the fruit was never intended for us. Sometimes our own personal growth was the fruit all along. Sometimes our actions, though seemingly huge in our eyes, are only a fragment of a big operation, and only after many people do small parts, do we see amazing things happen.

When God asks "future us" what we did with the opportunities he gave us, we will not want to stand before him without excuse, gazing at a heap of missed opportunities and unused talents meant for a planned purpose. But imagine the joy we will experience when we have accomplished our God-given tasks, pressed in to every opportunity we were given, and are told, "Well done, my good and faithful servant!" That is the expectation of a masterpiece!

Reflection: When have you felt a nudge from God and acted on it? What nudging have you felt but questioned or ignored until you missed the opportunity? What held you back? If the opportunity is still there, consider carrying it out now.

Prayer: God, thank you for purpose. Some days I wake up and grumble because there is so much work to do. Sometimes I feel exasperated when you request something of me. Forgive me for my wrong attitude. I know you fully equip me for the tasks you give me, including the energy, knowledge, wisdom, and ability. Help me to complete all you've called me to do today, nothing less. May nothing hold me back from the good works you have prepared beforehand for me to do. Amen.

Worship: "Here For A Reason" by Ashes Remain and "God Help Me" by Plumb

100

Breaking the Spiritual Rut

Sing to the Lord a new song.
Psalm 96:1

Have you ever heard a new worship song that resonated with your heart so much you couldn't get enough? Then, you played it over and over until it lost its initial meaning and impact? The same goes for prayers. "Pre-made" scripted prayers have their benefits as long as our hearts and minds are fully engaged. The prayers of others, those of faith who have gone before us, can prompt us to request things and thank God for things we may not have considered. They can lead us into thoughts about God that our minds haven't yet formulated. They also may help us realize we aren't alone in our struggles as others have shared similar experiences. These prayers have their time and place. In fact, the Bible itself is an abundant source of prayers from the hearts of people to God. However, scripted prayers when used too often, can become rote, cause us to lose mindfulness, and get us stuck in a rut with God. This was what Jesus was referring to when he condemned meaningless repetition in prayer (Matthew 6:7). This includes music. Much of our worship music is prayers to God through song.

Spiritual ruts are commonplace among believers. We all sink into them from time to time. Though a new spark may ignite in us to dive back into reading the Bible and praying, returning to the same thing over and over quenches our zeal, leaving us bored and lukewarm again. In other relationships, we know doing and saying the same things over and over prevent growth within the relationship. When time with our Creator has become mechanical, the God-given food for our soul is left on the table, and the reason for our being becomes completely lost. Our most important pursuit is null.

If you find your time with God has become stale, you've lost motivation, or are no longer enjoying time with God, it is time for a new song. To keep it fresh, try one or more of these:

- Include worship music. Pray the thoughts expressed in the songs. This is one of my favorite ways to spend time with God. Oftentimes, the lyrics lead me into deeper, more meaningful, prayer. Look for unfamiliar songs to "sing a new song."
- Journal using the SOAP method:
  - » Scripture: Write out your study verse or a verse that impacted you.
  - » Observation: Why did it impact you? What is God saying to you?
  - » Application: How does this verse apply to your life? In what ways do you want to grow or be changed by it?
  - » Prayer: After meditating on the verse, use it to guide your prayer. Ask God to help you grow and change by this new insight. Praying the Word is powerful and effective. Plus, when we pray the Word, we can have confidence our prayers are in line with his will.
- Write out your heartfelt needs and desires into a prayer. Read it with expectation each day.
- Write out a Psalm that expresses your heart. Personalize the Psalm from your own heart to God. The Psalms are saturated with various emotions—pain, joy, doubt, fear, anger—and express what we may have trouble articulating on our own. As the Psalms are songs, praying them is a great way to "sing a new song."
- Find a good devotional that rips right into your heart or a commentary which teaches you the history, culture, and context of certain Scriptures.
- Set up accountability. This can be done if you have a friend who wants to join you for a study on a Bible-sharing app. Choose a topic and invite some friends to join you in that study. Bible-sharing apps usually have a place to share thoughts from the study with one another.
- Commit to memorizing verses. Write them down in the morning on a sticky note and work on memorizing them while you're driving, folding laundry, cooking, etc… There is much information out there

on the best ways to memorize, including tips and tricks. Choose a method that works for you.

- Change positions as you pray—stand with arms high as you thank him, bow in reverence as you speak of his goodness, lay prostrate (face-down) as you confess your sins, get on your knees as you beg him to intervene in your life and the lives of others, raise your arms up again as you reach for his comfort, wrap a blanket around you as you envision his arms around you.
- Don't read quickly but grab hold of one verse that speaks to you and let it marinate. Apply it to your own life scenarios. A "read and run" robs us of the treasures buried in the Word.
- If you find your thoughts drifting off during prayer, try praying aloud. If that makes you uncomfortable, try whispering your prayer with instrumental music softly playing in the background.

Reflection: If you have already established a habit of quiet time, is it currently life-giving or has it become stagnant? Which ideas listed above interest you for reviving this time? What other ways can you think to "sing a new song"?

Prayer: God, thank you for always meeting me when I come to you. There are many times, you come to me and I don't give you the same courtesy. Forgive me for the times I place a higher priority on what I'm doing than on what you're saying to me. Forgive me for the times I've allowed our time together to become stale. Please breathe fresh air into our time and teach me to "sing a new song." I will look forward to our time together and protect it like the treasure it is. Amen.

Worship: "Fresh Fire" by Housefires and "Fresh Outpouring" by Jesus Culture

Conclusion

I hope you have learned so much through these studies, especially about God's love for you, his desire for intimacy with you, and his expectations for your life and relationships. May you experience Life in Abundance! My prayer is that God gripped you—like he gripped me—and reshaped your heart in an incredible, life-changing way. May you never stop learning, stretching, and growing.

If you enjoyed this devotional, be on the lookout for "Life In Abundance Book 2" in the near future.

Notes

1. Dietrich Bonhoeffer, *Temptation* (London: SCM Press Ltd, 1961), 33.

2. Susan Cheever, *A Woman's Life: The Story of an Ordinary American and Her Extraordinary Generation,* (New York: William Morrow and Company, 1994), 132-133.

3. Breazeale, Ron, "Thoughts, Neurotransmitters, Body-Mind Connection." *Psychology Today*. 17 July, 2012, https://www.psychologytoday.com/us/blog/in-the-face-adversity/201207/thoughts-neurotransmitters-body-mind-connection

4. Erickson, Thane M., et al. "Compassionate and Self-Image Goals as Interpersonal Maintenance Factors in Clinical Depression and Anxiety." *Journal of Clinical Psychology*. 74. 12 September 2017: 608-628. Epub. 27 June, 2022. https://pubmed.ncbi.nlm.nih.gov/28898407/

5. Billy Graham, "Inspirational Billy Graham Quotes About Faith." *Everyday Power*. 26 February, 2021. Accessed 27 June, 2022. https://everydaypower.com/billy-graham-quotes/ accessed 27 June 2022.

6. Thayer and Smith. "Greek Lexicon entry for Apaugasma." 2022. https://www.biblestudytools.com/lexicons/greek/kjv/apaugasma.html

7. "Seeing the dark—Editorials & Commentary—International Herald Tribune." *The New York Times*. 23 August, 2006. https://www.nytimes.com/2006/08/23/opinion/23iht-eddark.2570794.html. Accessed 27 June, 2022.

8. Starr, Eve. "Inside TV." *Greensboro Record*, Greensboro, North Carolina. November 4, 1954, Page B3, Column 4. GenealogyBank.

9. Piper, John. "Jesus Christ Egomaniac?" *Desiring God*. 29 July, 2016. https://www.desiringgod.org/messages/jesus-christ-egomaniac. 27 June, 2022

10. West, Kanye. Interview. Conducted by Sway in the Morning. 26 November, 2013.

11. Joni Eareckson Tada, *Place of Healing: Wrestling with the Mysteries of Suffering, Pain, and God's Sovereignty*, (Colorado Springs: David C. Cook, 2015), 67.

About the Author

Mandy Shrock is the founder of Marriage In Abundance, a ministry aimed at deepening the bonds of married couples. She is passionate about life, the Word of God, marriage, sci-fi and fantasy books, exercise, the outdoors, natural foods, and dogs. Powered by coffee, she lives with her husband, four children, and two dogs in northern Indiana.

Mandy Shrock directs Marriage In Abundance, a ministry which helps married couples strengthen their marriage bond by teaching them practical ways to deepen their connection, helping them communicate love to one another more effectively, and giving ideas to spice up their romance.

For more information, visit www.marriageinabundance.com.

www.ingramcontent.com/pod-product-compliance
Lightning Source LLC
Chambersburg PA
CBHW021705120626
46545CB00004B/1410